TEACHERS AS LEARNERS

EXEMPLARY TEACHERS'

PERCEPTIONS OF PERSONAL AND

PROFESSIONAL RENEWAL

VIVIENNE COLLINSON

TEACHERS AS LEARNERS

EXEMPLARY TEACHERS'

PERCEPTIONS OF PERSONAL AND

PROFESSIONAL RENEWAL

VIVIENNE COLLINSON

Austin & Winfield
San Francisco - London
1994

Library of Congress Cataloging-in-Publication Data

Collinson, Vivienne, 1949-
    Teachers as learners : exemplary teachers' perception of personal
and professional development / Vivienne Collinson.
        p. cm.
    Includes bibliographical references (p.) and index.
    ISBN 1-880921-79-0 : $59.95 -- ISBN 1-880921-78-2 (pbk.) : $39.95
    1. Teachers--United States--Cases studies. 2. Teachers--In-service
training--United States--Case studies. I. Title.
LB1776.2.C65 1994
372.11'00973--dc20   94-3924
                                                                   CIP

Editorial Inquiries:
Austin & Winfield, Publishers
P.O.Box 2590
San Francisco, CA 94126
(415) 981-5144

To Order: (800) 99-AUSTIN

To

Amy, Camille, Donna,

Elizabeth, Irene, and Mary

TABLE OF CONTENTS

LIST OF TABLES v

PREFACE vii

ACKNOWLEDGMENTS ix

CHAPTER   PAGE

I. INTRODUCTION 1
    Context of the Problem 1
    Statement of the Problem 3
    Significance of the Study 4
    An Overview of the Methodology 5
    Underlying Assumptions 5
    Definition of Terms 5
    Summary 6

II. REVIEW OF RELATED LITERATURE 7
    Individual Renewal/Organizational Renewal 7
    Gardner's Conceptualization of Self-Renewal 16
    Exemplary Teachers: A Neglected Resource
      in our Knowledge of Teacher Renewal 21
    Teacher Development 23
        An Expanded Definition of Professional Development 24
            Pedagogical development 24
            Understanding of self and others 24
            Cognitive development 25
            Theoretical development 25
            Professional development 26
            Career development 26
        Recent Trends in Teacher Development 26
        Teachers' Biographies 27
        Teachers as Adult Learners 28
    Organizational Climate 30
        Teachers' Workplace 32
            Shared goals 32
            Collaboration 32

i

Teacher certainty 33
Teacher commitment 33
Learning and Efficacy 33
Commitment 34
Collaboration and Collegiality 35
Conclusion 38
Summary 39

III. METHODOLOGY 41
Rationale for Qualitative Research 41
The Case Study Method 42
The Researcher's Role 43
Data Collection 44
Selection of Participants 44
Interviews 46
Instruments 47
Data Analysis 48
Procedure 48
Trustworthiness.. 49
Triangulation... 50
Validity.. 51
A Caveat Concerning Exemplary Teachers 52
Summary 54

IV. FINDINGS... 55
"Impressionistic" Sketches of the Teacher Participants 56
Mary.. 56
Elizabeth 56
Irene 57
Amy 57
Camille... 57
Donna... 58
Formative Experiences 58
School Days 58
A Work Ethic 64
Discussion 64
Becoming a Teacher 65
Distinctive Preservice Experiences 65
Common Experiences as Beginning Teachers....................................... 66

Teaching at Maplewood School 67
Open space, team teaching, and observation 67
Discussion 72
Beliefs About Teaching/Learning 73
On Teaching and Learning 73
In-Between-the-Lines Teaching 76
Adjusting Curriculum to Contexts 79
Adjusting Assessment to Beliefs about Learning 81
Teaching Beyond the Classroom 83
Discussion 85
Personal and Professional Renewal 87
Personal Renewal 87
Professional Renewal 88
Renewal and social interaction 89
Reflection 91
Reading recovery training 92
Scope of involvement 93
A credibility gap 96
Discussion 97
Factors Enabling and/or Constraining Renewal 99
Personal Factors 99
Professionalism 103
Collegiality 104
Balancing an imbalance of power 105
Leadership and teacher renewal 107
Collegial networks and career development 108
Transfers: A Search for Enabling Renewal 109
Principal/teacher dimensions 110
Teacher/teacher dimensions 112
Resources and District Support 114
Dealing with Constraints 116
Discussion 117
An Ethic of Care 119
Rewards 121
Discussion 122
Commitment 123
Decisions about Teaching 124
Discussion 126
Ideal Visions for Teachers' Professional Development 126

    Discussion 128
    Summary 129
V. IMPLICATIONS AND SUGGESTIONS FOR
    FURTHER RESEARCH 131
    Teacher Selection 132
        An Argument for Academic Ability and Dispositions 132
        Use of Teachers' Dispositions and Biographies in Teacher Selection.... 133
            Teachers' dispositions 133
            Teachers' biographies 134
            Teacher "image" and early success in teaching 135
            Teachers as recruiting agents 136
    Teacher Education 136
        A Focus on What Teachers Need to Learn 136
            Inquiry and human interaction as a focus of teacher education 137
            Inservice teacher education 139
    Creating Desirable Contexts for Self-Renewal 140
    Suggestions for Further Research 142
        Exemplary Teachers 142
        Teacher Commitment and Retention 143
    Conclusion 143

APPENDICES 144
    A. Nomination Form 144
    B. Guided Interview Schedules 145
    C. Professional Development Activities for Teachers 148
    D. Table D-1: Results from the OCDQ-RE Questionnaire 150

NOTES 152

BIBLIOGRAPHY 153

INDEX 171

LIST OF TABLES

TABLE   PAGE

1. A summary of literature: Self-Renewing
   individuals and supportive organizations 9

D-1.   Results from the OCDQ-RE questionnaire 149

PREFACE

As a novice classroom teacher, I often wondered why some colleagues remained enthusiastic about their work while others did not and why some teachers, but not all, were implicitly or explicitly recognized as exemplary by their peers. Surely, I thought, there must be specific exemplary behaviors that all teachers could learn. The thought of an exemplary teacher in every classroom was tantalizing, especially at a time when simplistic formulas and standard operating procedures were proffered as panaceas for improving education. Yet the only common denominator among the exemplary teachers I had known as a student or colleague seemed to be that they all kept learning. They learned in myriad ways and about topics not necessarily connected to their professional work. What had made these teachers learners? How did they pursue learning while they were so busy teaching? How did learning about gardens or gastronomics help them as teachers?

Years later, as a doctoral student, I came back to the question that had dogged me for so many years. I quickly discovered that our knowledge of how teachers learn and develop is quite limited, as is the research on exemplary teachers and on organizational factors that enable and/or constrain teacher renewal. Assuming, like Sophocles, that "the reasonable thing is to learn from those who can teach", I decided to investigate the personal and professional renewal of teachers nominated as exemplary by their peers.

My review of the literature led me to John Gardner's conceptualization of self-renewal and the parallel ideas and ideals in the literatures on exemplary teachers, teacher development, and organizational climate. The six veteran participants in the study spoke readily about their family's work ethic and attitude toward education, their early teacher role models, formative experiences, professional activities, personal renewal, the factors that have most enabled them to remain teacher learners, and their ideal vision for teachers' professional development.

Over and over, I heard the clearly articulated strength and passion of their beliefs about teaching and learning and so, wanting to give the teachers "pride of place", I created an experimental text (Chapter 4) in which the participants "converse" though they never met. I was moved and puzzled by stories that directly and indirectly describe care and commitment; puzzled because the teachers' stories suggest that these two areas are far more important and interrelated than we may have thought previously.

Above all, this inquiry revealed the complexity of dispositional and contextual factors affecting teachers' work and learning. The results indicate that if we want self-renewing excellent teachers, we need to understand their means of renewal, as well as their attributes and dispositions, and then seek and support environments that encourage them to excel as teachers and learners.

ACKNOWLEDGMENTS

There are many people to whom I owe my deepest gratitude for their friendship, advice, and support throughout my doctoral program at The Ohio State University. Specifically, I would like to extend my thanks to my dissertation committee, Elsie Alberty, Robert Donmoyer, Kenneth Howey, and Nancy Zimpher for their encouragement, confidence, and stimulating classes. Most of all, I would like to thank my advisor, Kenneth Howey, for his wisdom, invaluable questions, and many challenges that helped me think more deeply and clarify positions.

I am also indebted to the Federation of Women Teachers' Associations of Ontario for the 1990 L. Dorothy Martin Doctoral Scholarship, as well as the support of Joan Westcott and my teachers of the provincial leadership course who were strong role models for me. Finally, my sincere appreciation and admiration of the six exemplary teachers who participated in this study. Their depth of knowledge, caring, and commitment is inspiring.

CHAPTER I
INTRODUCTION

Context of the Problem

The reasonable thing is to learn from those who can teach.

Sophocles

During the decade of the eighties, various themes related to "excellence" emerged. Two best-selling books quickly caught the attention of the public: *In Search of Excellence* (Peters and Waterman, 1982) and *Theory Z* (Ouchi, 1981), a new theory for the achievement of excellence based on the assumption that a worker's life is a whole. Both treatises concentrated on the power of workplace culture to stimulate workers' growth and satisfaction. Together, they created a major shift in the direction of research on organizational climate, an extremely complex interaction of many factors: culture (norms, belief systems, values); ecology (physical/material factors such as technology or size of the building); milieu (areas such as motivation and morale of individuals and groups); and organizational structure (Owens, 1991). At the same time in education, *A Nation at Risk* (National Commission on Excellence in Education, 1983) expressed concern over declining excellence in American schools while Goodlad (1984) and Sizer (1984) drew our attention to the crushing dailyness and dreary routines of teaching.

The Carnegie Task Force on Teaching as a Profession (1986) and publications by the Holmes Group (1986, 1990) focussed on the quality of preservice teachers and the professionalization of teaching as a way to increase the knowledge, qualifications, and status of teachers. Solutions included attracting high academic graduates and retaining them by creating new leadership positions in a traditionally "flat" career (Lortie, 1975). Experienced teachers were, at this time, becoming increasingly familiar with the term "burnout" as researchers concentrated on the shortcomings of "deficient" teachers, almost ignoring their exemplary colleagues.

In a search for educational excellence, however, it seems logical to begin by studying exemplary teachers who manage to excel while working in the same districts or schools as their colleagues who "burn out" or leave teaching. Yet the literature on exemplary teachers is extremely limited and much of it has focussed on their characteristics (Dieter, 1975; Easterly, 1983; Van Schaack and Glick, 1982), of which three tend to cut acRoss all descriptions of exemplary teachers: a love of learning, an ethic of care, and commitment to teaching

In terms of these three characteristics, exemplary teachers' desire and motivation to learn and grow is paramount (also see Mertz, 1987 and Wigginton, 1985). Their love of learning has earned them the descriptors of "continual learners" (Easterly, 1983) and "total omnivores" constantly striving for personal growth (Joyce, Hersh, and McKibbin, 1983), exhibiting "a deep concern for professional development" in an endless quest to be better teachers (Van Schaack and Glick, 1982).

While this characteristic is repeatedly underscored, just exactly how exemplary teachers pursue learning throughout their career has been only marginally addressed. For example, Penick, Yager, and Bonstetter (1986) noted that expert teachers of exemplary science programs had completed more years of graduate work than their colleagues and were active in professional organizations. Joyce, Hersh, and McKibbin (1983) recognized that the teachers characterized as total omnivores creatively sought out resources, colleagues, and improvement possibilities. These two studies revealed general ways exemplary teachers pursue professional growth.

There was however, in the same decade, a growing concern over the separation of a "whole person" into two distinct and unconnected lives: the professional and the personal. Researchers such as Ball and Goodson (1985), Woods (1986), and Zeichner and Grant (1981) argued that the biography or prior knowledge of teachers influences their beliefs and actions, a claim made earlier by Lortie (1975). In other words, teachers' personal and professional lives are interwoven and cannot be adequately understood separately: Why exemplary teachers believe and behave in particular ways could be better understood by including models and influences and life experiences that shape their attitudes and actions.

It remains clear that, in the accounts they give about life in schools, teachers constantly refer to personal and biographical factors. From their point of view, it would seem that professional practices are embedded in wider life concerns. We need to listen closely to their views on the relationship between "school life" and "whole life" for in that dialectic crucial tales about careers and commitments will be told. (Goodson, 1992, p. 16)

In a phenomenological study of significant life experiences of "Teachers of the Year" (Stone, 1987), the data supported the "premise that there is a relationship between the 'self' of the teacher and effective teaching" (p. 139). Again, the characteristics of dedication (commitment), genuine caring for others, and innovation emerged as the three most common attributes of these effective teachers (p. 117).

Still other researchers were examining the impact of the workplace on teachers. Rosenholtz (1989) documented the link between school cultures and teacher learning. Teachers who continued to learn and who were quick to seize opportunities for growth saw their own learning reflected in their students' learning. Positive student learning led to further teacher innovation and an increased sense of efficacy. Both teacher learning and student learning had earlier been found to be powerful rewards for high-performing teachers (Stevenson, 1986). Yee (1990) also noted the influence of school culture on teacher efficacy and commitment.

Collegial interaction, evident in "learning enriched" environments (Little, 1982; Rosenholtz, 1989), was valued by exemplary teachers and crucial to their involvement in and commitment to teaching (Stevenson, 1986). The exemplary teachers in a study by Campbell (1988) confirmed the importance of expert teachers developing collegial relationships with peers who share a desire to learn, who share ideas, and who support their decisions to "ignore, justify, or dismiss any aspect of the external work environment which interfered with their teaching mission" (p. 56). The important connection between teacher development and the school culture was summarized by McLaughlin and Yee (1988):

> Investment in teachers -- attention to their long-range growth needs -- prevents burnout and reduced involvement by providing jobs with a high level of opportunity and power. It also means creating a work environment that is resource-adequate, integrated, collegial, and problem-solving -- in other words, an environment in which a teacher can have a rewarding career. (p. 39)

Statement of the Problem

This study builds on the above research by investigating exemplary teachers' personal and professional renewal throughout their career and selected factors that have enabled and/or constrained their renewal. The purpose of the study is to contextualize the renewal of exemplary teachers and in doing so, to broaden understanding of teachers as learners.

Research indicates that exemplary teachers share various characteristics, including a desire for continuous renewal. Biographical studies of teachers' lives demonstrate that these characteristics or dispositions have been established to varying degrees before teachers begin their professional career. What is unclear is *how* exemplary teachers self-renew personally and professionally throughout their teaching career. As Fullan and Hargreaves (1992) point out, not only have teachers as persons been neglected in studies on teacher development, but much of this inquiry has also failed to value and involve veteran teachers (p. 5).

Since prior studies indicated that exemplary teachers continue to be influenced by their workplace environment, this line of thinking led to another question: Which factors enable and/or constrain teachers' renewal? Specifically, then, the questions that framed the study were:

1. What are exemplary teachers' beliefs about teaching/learning and are these related to their renewal?
2. How do exemplary teachers self-renew personally and professionally?
3. Is there an expanding scope of professional awareness, involvement, and contribution throughout their career? (e.g., classroom, school, district, state, national, international)
4. Which personal and contextual factors enable and/or constrain their renewal?
5. How do exemplary teachers deal with constraints on their renewal?
6. What are their visions for improving professional development for teachers?

Significance of the Study

In the eighties, although there was a general focus on excellence in education, only a small number of researchers studied exemplary teachers. More attention was paid to teachers who left teaching because of burnout than to those who continued to excel in the same school districts. A better understanding of exemplary teachers may hold clues about personal and/or organizational factors that contribute to the retention of teachers.

During the same decade, the Carnegie Task Force on Teaching as a Profession (1986) and the Holmes Group (1986; 1990) concentrated on the quality of preservice teachers and the professionalization of teaching as a way to increase the knowledge, qualifications, and status of teachers although formative experiences and professional renewal undertaken by exemplary teachers in their quest for knowledge were not mentioned. Examination of the latters' biographies and renewal, as well as organizational factors enabling their renewal, may provide insights for improving teacher selection, preservice and inservice teacher education, and contexts in which teachers can excel. All three have potential to encourage the development of exemplary teachers.

An Overview of the Methodology

This qualitative case study included six participants: They are female, veteran elementary school teachers in an urban setting who were nominated by colleagues as exemplary teachers. The primary method of data collection was in-depth guided interviews. The teachers also responded to a questionnaire (Hoy, Tarter, and Kottkamp, 1991) examining teachers' perceptions of school climate. Themes and categories emerging from the data analysis, as well as interpretation of the data, were discussed with four peer debriefers. Accuracy of the participants' meaning and the proffered interpretations were verified through three member checks with each participant.

Underlying Assumptions

1. Teaching is a moral endeavor (e.g., Goodlad, Soder, and Sirotnik, 1990; Sergiovanni, 1992). How teachers teach reflects the values and beliefs they hold about teaching and learning.
2. If much learning occurs through social interaction with others, then self-renewing teachers have figured out ways of overcoming the "isolation" long associated with teaching (Ellis, 1984; Lortie, 1975; Sarason, 1971).
3. Studying how exemplary teachers engage in professional development and listening to what they consider valuable learning can be a point of departure for better understanding of teacher development.
4. Teacher commitment is strengthened through professional development opportunities that make their work meaningful.

Definition of Terms

Cooperating teacher. Sometimes referred to as associate teachers, these are experienced classroom teachers who work with preservice teachers assigned to schools as part of their field-based program.

Disposition. Katz and Raths (1985) define a disposition "as an attributed characteristic of a teacher, one that summarizes the trend of a teacher's actions in particular contexts. . . . The acts that constitute a disposition may be conscious and deliberate or so habitual and 'automatic' that they seem intuitive or spontaneous" (p. 301). The authors give illustrations such as a disposition to consider alternative interpretations, to seek help with one's teaching from others or the literature, to distinguish between what is said and what is meant, and to experiment (p. 302).

Elementary schools. For the purpose of this study, elementary schools include kindergarten through fifth grade.

Exemplary. The term "exemplary" is described variously as emulative, praise-worthy, noteworthy, worthy of imitation (Family Word Finder, 1975) or of serving as a model (Webster's Third New International Dictionary, 1976). In a review of the literature, synonymous terms included "outstanding" (Dieter, 1975; Easterly, 1983; Jackson, 1968/1990), "gifted" (Dewey, 1929), "high-performing" (Stevenson, 1986), "superior" (Ellett, Loup, Evans, and Chauvin, 1992), "expert" (Campbell, 1988), "talented" (Murphy, 1985), and "superlative" (Van Schaack and Glick, 1982). In choosing the term "exemplary" and thus expanding the list of labels, I tried to avoid possible vagueness and misunderstanding of terms such as "gifted," "talented," and "expert." I also wanted to avoid words like "superlative" and "superior" that connote a competitive or hierarchical ranking.

Peer debriefer. As one way to try to ensure accuracy of understanding and interpretation of the data, I worked with four full-time urban teachers who are also part-time graduate students. They volunteered to read parts of the raw data, critique my interpretations, and make suggestions.

Renewal. Bolin (1987) has described renewal as "making new again," "growing afresh," or "becoming new through growth" (pp. 13-14). In this study, personal renewal usually refers to "growing afresh" or refreshing oneself (e.g., listening to music or exercising as a change of pace or for quiet reflection). Professional renewal refers to job-related activities with the potential to contribute to "becoming new through growth" or "making new again." Growth, change, learning, and renewal are used almost synonymously. For the purpose of this study, renewal and self-renewal are virtually interchangeable, with self-renewal indicating more self-determination of the direction the renewal activities take. However, both terms imply positive change.

Professional development. Unless stated otherwise, professional development refers to any activity teachers engage in to inform or improve their practice.

Urbanville. This term refers to all urban districts.

Summary

Chapter 1 outlined the context of the problem, stated the problem and research questions, summarized the significance of the study, provided a brief overview of the methodology, and explained the underlying assumptions and definition of terms. Chapter 2 presents a review of related literature.

CHAPTER II
REVIEW OF RELATED LITERATURE

Just as Marie Clay (1991) studied good readers to help develop a theory of literacy and find out how to assist readers using unsuccessful strategies, I surmised that we could study exemplary teachers to help us move forward in our understanding of the complex task called teaching. Clay argues that social contexts have "a controlling influence on children's opportunities to learn" but that it is an examination of "active learners *changing over time* within their contexts" and how they use those opportunities to learn that indicate their construction of inner control over literacy (pp. 1-2). Similarly, I was interested in examining exemplary teachers' careers to find out how their social contexts influence renewal and, by extension, their teaching over time.

Individual Renewal/Organizational Renewal

Dewey (1938) wrote: "Mankind likes to think in terms of extreme opposites. It is given to formulating its beliefs in terms of *Either-Ors*, between which it recognizes no intermediate possibilities. . . . The history of educational theory is marked by opposition between the idea that education is development from within and that it is formation from without" (p. 17). That debate continues to pervade discussions about professional development or education for teachers.

St. Maurice (1990) pointed out that in research on staff development, there is division among those who see the individual teacher as agent and those who believe that schools are the most logical agents of change. Goodlad (1983) proposed that the individual school is a promising possibility as the key unit for educational improvement (p. 55) and that a satisfying workplace may be a necessity for "maintaining a productive educational environment" (p. 59). Little (1982) concurred: "Without denying differences in individuals' skills, interests, commitment, curiosity, or persistence, the prevailing pattern of interactions and interpretations in each [school] building demonstrably creates certain possibilities and sets certain limits" (p. 338).

Rosenholtz (1989) documented the link between teachers' learning as individuals and the contexts in which they work. Yee (1990) concluded that the degree and direction of teachers' professional involvement and commitment "are the product of experiences in the workplace, not simply the outcome of individual predisposition or personality" (p. 118). She noted that the balance between the two is very fragile, suggesting that the school climate can undermine or destroy high involvement and commitment (p. 118).

Even though the Rosenholtz study (1989) underscored the need for teachers to learn in a nurturing environment, Sarason (1990) contended that schools have remained intractable to change in part because they do not exist equally for the development of both students and teachers. The learning for *both* teachers and students must be meaningful. The link between teacher renewal and school culture has led other researchers as well to the conclusion that teacher development and school improvement are inseparable (Gibbons and Norman, 1987; Kemmis, 1987; Watson and Fullan, 1992). This was also the conclusion John Gardner (1963/1981) drew: that renewal of individuals and renewal of societies or organizations are simply two sides of the same coin. For an organization to achieve renewal, "it will have to be a hospitable environment for creative men and women. It will also have to produce men and women with the capacity for self-renewal" (p. xv). "Unless we foster versatile, innovative and self-renewing men and women, all the ingenious social arrangements in the world will not help us" (p. xvi).

Both knowledge of teachers as individuals and knowledge of the contexts in which exemplary teachers work inform this study. The review of the literature therefore is structured around exemplary teachers, teacher development, and the organizational climate of schools. However, the overarching conceptual framework for this study is the work on self-renewal by John Gardner (1963/1981). His conceptualization of self-renewal provides a foundation for understanding the relationships between exemplary teachers and the school environment, as well as between seemingly tenuously linked descriptors like renewal and motivation, growth and creativity, social interaction and risk taking. (See Table 1 for a summary of these literatures.)

Table 1

A Summary of Literature: Self-Renewing Individuals and Supportive Organizations

Literature	Continuous Learning	An Ethic of Care	Commitment to Teaching
Self-Renewal (Gardner, 1963/1981)	**Evidence of continuous learning:** • a system for continuous renewal	**Evidence of an ethic of care:** • fruitful relations with other people	**Commitment:** • strong motivation to be involved in something about which one cares deeply
	• inquiry	• accepting and giving love	• grounded in "striving toward meaningful goals--goals that relate the individual to a larger context of purposes . . . conceptions of the universe that give dignity, purpose and sense to our own existence" (pp. 97; 102)
	• complex decision making	• empathy for others	
	• self-knowledge	• dependability	
	• courage to risk failure	**Caring:** • enriches lives	
	• critical thinking	• dissolves rigidities of the isolated self	

Table 1 (continued)

Literature	Continuous Learning	An Ethic of Care	Commitment to Teaching
Self-Renewal (Gardner, 1963/1981) (continued)	• conservation by innovation • lifelong process of self-knowledge • development of capacities for sensing, wondering, loving, understanding, and aspiring • curiosity, open-mindedness • respect for evidence • creativity	• forces new perspectives, alters judgments • keeps the emotional substratum in working order	
Exemplary Teachers	**Evidence of continuous learning:** • deep concern for professional development (Van Schaack & Glick, 1982) • love of learning (Easterly, 1983; Mertz, 1987; Penick, Yager, & Bonstetter, 1986; Wigginton, 1985) genuine concern for students	**Evidence of a caring teacher:** • willing to give of oneself (Van Schaack & Glick, 1982) (Stone, 1987; Van Schaack & Glick, 1982) • global perspective (Mertz, 1987)	**Evidence of commitment:** • renews self and seeks to improve teaching (Mertz, 1987; Shanoski & Hranitz, 1989; Stone, 1987; Van Schaack & Glick, 1982) • risk taking (Mertz, 1987; Van Schaack & Glick, 1982)

Table 1 (continued)

Literature	Continuous Learning	An Ethic of Care	Commitment to Teaching
• high sense of efficacy	Schaack & Glick, 1982) • deeply involved; builds relation- 1987) • excellent communicator (Easterly, • dedicated (Easterly, 1983) • flexibility; open-mindedness • humane and tolerant (Campbell, 1988 (Campbell, 1988; Stevenson, 1986) (Campbell, 1988; Stevenson, 1986) • considers human interactions autonomy (Campbell, 1988) • loves seeing student growth	ships (Wigginton, 1985) • balanced perspective of world and 1983; Shanoski & Hranitz, 1989) • active in professional organizations (Easterly, 1983) • creativity (Stone, 1987) • seeks high-performing colleagues Exemplary Teachers (continued) **Associated with:** • rewarding (Stevenson, 1986) • strong sense of professional (Campbell, 1988) Teacher Development	• own place in it (Stone, 1987) • innovation (Easterly, 1983; Stone, (Penick, Yager, & Bonstetter, 1986) • intellectual curiosity (Easterly, 1983)

Table 1 (continued)

Literature	Continuous Learning	An Ethic of Care	Commitment to Teaching
Continuous learning:	• self in continuous formation (Dewey, 1916/1966) **Ethic of care requires:**	• community to support risks (Huebner, 1987) **Motivation:**	• rooted in curiosity, wonder (Dewey, 1916; Dewey 1933; Green, 1971) necessary for individual and school
	• improvement (Gibbons & Norman, 1987; Kemmis, 1987; Talbert, 1993; Watson & Fullan, 1992) • openness and vulnerability	(Huebner, 1987) **Commitment:**	• to personal growth and improving teaching (Joyce, Hersh, & McKibbin, 1983; Leithwood, 1990) a paradox of human need to grow
	• and to conserve (Joyce, 1984) **Associated with:**	• human connections and risk (Greene, 1987; Lieberman, Saxl, & Miles, 1988) • a sustaining force (Heath, 1980)	• job-embedded (Yarger, Howey, &
	Joyce, 1980 • reward; interaction with respected	colleagues (McLaughlin & Yee, 1988) • demands risk (Bolin, 1987;	
	• Valencia & Killion, 1988 • intrinsic reward: "making a	difference" (Lortie, 1975) **Associated with:**	
	• disposition to seek alternatives (Heath, 1980; Howey, 1985; Resnick & Klopfer, 1989) • higher cognitive and moral	development (Thies-Sprinthall & Sprinthall, 1983) Teacher Development (continued)	

Table 1 (continued)

Literature	Continuous Learning	An Ethic of Care	Commitment to Teaching
• disposition of keen sense of	curiosity, high degree of intellectual honesty, healthy skepticism (Jackson, 1987) • high psychological development 1985; Leithwood, 1990) • good teaching/learning (Heath, (Howey, 1985) • certainty of ability to solve prob- lems (Heath, 1980) **Curiosity:** • sparks inquiry (Dewey, 1933) • encourages risk taking (Joyce, 1984) Organizational Climate	(Heath, 1980; Leithwood, 1990) reflection (Heath, 1980; Howey, 1980; Willie & Howey, 1980) systematic inquiry and judgment	

Table 1 (continued)

Literature	Continuous Learning	An Ethic of Care	Commitment to Teaching
Continuous learning:	• stimulates further renewal (Rosenholtz, 1989) **Relationships with adults:** 1990) • stimulating professional interaction (Rosenholtz, 1989; Smylie, 1990) • support system encourages risk (see (Little, 1992) **Relationships with students:** (Sarason, 1990) • may be misunderstood as choice to • innovation and professional interaction (Little, 1982) **Human relationships:** 1989) • contribute to school health (Hoy,	• respect from relevant adults desired (Louis & Smith, 1990) **Motivation:** with peers rewarding (Kanter, 1981; Louis & Smith, 1990) • necessary for commitment Stoll, 1992) **Commitment:** • and good teaching (Ashton & Webb, 1986; Hargreaves, 1993) • strengthened by task autonomy be isolated (Hargreaves, 1993) **Associated with:** • and meaningful feedback important for high performance (Rosenholtz, 1989) • high sense of efficacy (Rosenholtz, Tarter, & Kottkamp, 1991) • risk taking (see Stoll, 1992)	• seriously oversimplified (Lieberman & Rosenholtz, 1987) calls for self-knowledge (Smylie, (Rosenholtz, 1989) • improves student learning • requires learning opportunities (Rosenholtz, 1989) Organizational Climate (continued) (Rosenholtz, 1989) • required of teacher and student

Table 1 (continued)

Literature	Continuous Learning	An Ethic of Care	Commitment to Teaching
• more successful if job-embedded	• human interaction (Ashton & Webb, 1986; McLaughlin & Marsh, 1978; Rosenholtz, 1989) **Efficacy:** • and teacher certainty (Rosenholtz, 1989) • linked to innovation, risk, and participation in decision making (McLaughlin & Marsh, 1978; Rosenholtz, 1989; Smylie, 1990)		

Gardner's Conceptualization of Self-Renewal

In his book, *Self-Renewal: The Individual and the Innovative Society*, Gardner (1963/1981) elaborates principles concerning the self-renewing individual. His explanation paints a portrait of ideal characteristics of persons intensely interested in the process of lifelong learning. He posits that self-renewing individuals will show evidence of a system for continuous renewal, inquiry and complex decision making, self-knowledge, the courage to risk failure, fruitful relations with other people, critical thinking, and a strong motivation to be involved in something about which they care deeply. These qualities will be discussed separately although together, they form a consistent whole, a way of thinking.

First, the self-renewing person has developed a maturing "system or framework within which continuous innovation, renewal and rebirth can occur" (p. 5). To describe this framework, Gardner uses the metaphor of a balanced ecological system where, within the same system, some things are being born at the same time that others are flourishing and still others are dying (p. 5). The same metaphor is used in *The Ecology of School Renewal* (Goodlad,1987). The idea is also similar to three functions of teacher education outlined by Schlechty and Whitford (1983):

1. the *establishing* function (introduction of new programs, technologies, or procedures);
2. the *enhancement* function (expanding knowledge, enhancing performance capacities, refining existing skills);
3. the *maintenance* function (assuring compliance with routines, supporting preferred modes of operating, protecting from outside influence). (p. 77)

It seems, then, that self-renewal requires the first two processes of change to balance the third process which represents some kind of stasis or stability. It is the balance within the system or framework that represents growing maturity: One is not fearfully hanging on to the known and comfortable while refusing to change, but nor is one overwhelmed by innovations with no secure foundation. However, the metaphor also suggests that individuals are part of much larger, interrelated systems and cannot be divorced from those contexts. That is, a certain amount of continuity is required for balance even as innovations are taking place. Gardner takes pains to explain that shared purposes of a society appear at first to be a maintenance function or major element of continuity, but that it is through constant reappraisal that they remain relevant and vital (p. 22).

Second, the self-renewing person has a process of bringing the results of change into line with long-term purposes and values (Gardner, 1963/1981, p. 6). The process is a complex interweaving of continuity and change, conservation by innovation, stability in motion (p. 7). Gardner uses the example of a scientist who may easily discard a theory but who will become angry if a favorite pipe is thrown out. The important point is that continuity and change exist side by side; continuity is only problematic when it interferes with renewal and innovation, when it prevents us from seeing fresh perspectives. "There is in anyone's normal environment enough depth and variety of human experience, enough complexity of human interaction to place endlessly new demands on the mind and spirit — provided one has within oneself the gift for constantly searching one's small universe" (p. 130).

This is the same contradiction that Joyce (1984) describes in discussing the discomfort of learning. "The need to grow is built into the fiber of our being. . . . Paradoxically, however, we have an ingrained tendency to conserve our beings as they are or were" (p. 33). Real growth requires disequilibrium instead of comfort; problems and diverse opinions challenge fixed attitudes (p. 34). Another way of putting this is that the self-renewing individual, in continually looking for opportunities or new ways of identifying, thinking about, or solving problems, has developed a disposition for thinking and applying knowledge (Resnick and Klopfer, 1989, p. 7). The habit of seeking alternative solutions prevents rigidity and a dependence on maintenance of the familiar or status quo while allowing change to be systematic instead of a cacophony of fads. Thus "the self is not something ready-made, but something in continuous formation through choice of action." (Dewey, 1916/1966, p. 351)

It seems, then, that one way to cope with change and achieve some semblance of balance is to recognize that neither the individual's nor the organization's vitality and development can be left to chance; it must be a systematic and continuous development with a framework of carefully examined values.

> The purpose of education is to generate the conditions that will enable us to acknowledge the disequilibrium of change as a fundamental of the continuance of growth so that we can reach beyond ourselves toward a richer understanding and accept the wisdom that lies within ourselves, which is that discomfort is our lot if we are not to be arrested along our road." (Joyce, 1984, p. 34)

If schools do not encourage a disposition for thinking and for applying knowledge, if they do not have a process for bringing change into line with long term values, it should not surprise us that non-renewing teachers and schools would be resistant to change (e.g., Sarason, 1990). Refrains of "If it ain't broke, don't fix it" and "This too shall pass" are reflections of individuals and school systems that have blocked their capacity to renew and adapt to a world that does not stand still. They have put too Little emphasis on developing dispositions and systems that facilitate change and too much emphasis on stability or maintenance. Such teachers and schools are being pushed and pulled to change, but have not established the cultures and dispositions that strengthen and enrich renewal.

Third, Gardner (1963/1981) posits that self-renewing individuals undertake a lifelong process of self-discovery and self-knowledge. They systematically seek to develop "the full range of [their] capacities for sensing, wondering, learning, understanding, loving and aspiring" (pp. 11-12). Gardner is not alone in linking self-knowledge to learning or development. In a review of the literature, Howey (1985) notes that one of the functions of staff development should be the understanding and discovery of self (discussed later).

Fourth, the self-renewing individual has the courage to risk failure in order to learn (Gardner, 1963/1981, p. 14). This represents as great a paradox as the need to grow and the desire to conserve discussed above. The paradox here is that learning requires individuals to risk failure although they are schooled to see failure as a lack of learning. Several other authors have noticed the important relationship between learning and the courage to risk failure. Bolin (1987) reminds us that renewal includes the idea of "growing afresh. . . . Associated with freshness and growth are change and repair. To change and repair, the teacher must, again, face risk. Without the risk of change, one may not be able to discover some new fresh thing or be able to renew a fight. . . . Such freshness is possible every time the teacher faces a new class of students, if the teacher recognizes that there is openness to knowledge and open possibilities in every relationship" (pp. 14-15).

Huebner (1987) expands this understanding of risk: "Teachers must act in an imperfect world. To postpone action until the knowledge and technique makers establish the educational millennium is sheer irresponsibility, based on illusions of progress. We have no choice but to risk ourselves. The choice is to consider the risk private or to build a community that accepts vulnerability and shares risks. Vulnerability is endurable in a community of care and support — a community in which members take time telling and listening to the stories of each other's journey" (p. 26). Maxine Greene (1987), citing a literary essay by De Mott, again picks up the threads linking risk taking, vulnerability, human interactions, and renewal: "[W]riters (like the rest of us) have to feel forward — live forward a l little, risk more in the name of full human connection — to become what they can become and to renew life for others" (p. 180).

Fifth, another attribute already alluded to is the ability of self-renewing individuals to have "mutually fruitful relations" with other human beings (Gardner, 1963/1981, p. 15). They are able to accept and give love, have empathy for others, depend on others and can be depended upon. Healthy social interactions enrich their lives. "Love and friendship dissolve the rigidities of the isolated self, force new perspectives, alter judgments and keep in working order the emotional substratum on which all profound comprehension of human affairs must rest" (p. 16). Since teaching depends on human interaction, one might expect self-renewing teachers to exhibit high levels of fruitful relations with others.

Sixth, self-renewing individuals have developed "habits of mind that will be useful in new situations — curiosity, open-mindedness, objectivity, respect for evidence and the capacity to think critically" (p. 23). As early as 1963, Gardner was calling for education that would deepen understanding, strengthen performance, emphasize analysis, and encourage problem solving — the habits of good thinking Dewey (1933/1960) embraced and the kind of education research in cognitive science would support (e.g., Gardner, 1991; Resnick and Klopfer, 1989). Jackson (1987), in discussing the phrase "learning to learn," also refers to dispositions and cognition.

> In cognitive terms, this means teaching a person to reason, to make judgments, to develop sustained arguments, to criticize the arguments of others, and so forth. . . . In terms more dispositional than cognitive, it means equipping the would-be learner with those attitudinal and emotional attributes . . . that predispose a person to the use of reason. These include a keen sense of curiosity, a high degree of intellectual honesty, self-confidence in one's ability to acquire knowledge, a healthy degree of skepticism when confronted with the knowledge claims of others, and so forth. . . . Taken together, these two components of learning to learn, the cognitive and the dispositional, add up to a readily recognizable intellectual posture. (p. 49)

The final attribute of the self-renewing individual is the motivation to do "something about which he [sic] cares deeply" (Gardner, 1963/1981, p. 17). Motivation "is an attribute of individuals, in part linked to their physical vitality, in part a resultant of social forces — patterns of child-rearing, the tone of the educational system, presence or absence of opportunity, the tendency of the society to release or smother available energy, social attitudes toward dedication or commitment and the vitality of the society's shared values" (p. 19). Green (1971) links motivation to wonder:

> When curiosity is rooted in a sense of wonder, then reflection and study become not tasks, but necessities — as spontaneous and essential for life as breathing. . . . This is the consuming and pervasive motivation which teachers should aspire to in themselves and long for in their students. It will not be cultivated by devices or by frantic innovations. A change of curriculum is not the sufficient condition for it. Nor will it be accomplished by a more rigorous application of learning theory or by wearisome conferences and

workshops. . . . The thirst for learning shall not be cultivated by a fearful and anxiety-ridden search for shortcuts. It shall begin to take form when we evidence patient and calm discovery of the wonders of this world and a corresponding capacity to marvel at them. (p. 202)

Dewey (1916/1966; 1933/1960) believed that motivation or interests must be channeled into habits of discipline and thinking, but that an attitude of curiosity or wonder is vital to the process. "Until we understand, we are, if we have curiosity, troubled, baffled, and hence moved to inquire" (1933/1960, p. 132). "Unless transition to an intellectual plane is effected, curiosity degenerates or evaporates" (p. 39). Curiosity seems to play a vital role in creating "dynamic disequilibrium" (Joyce, 1984) and an openness to taking risks.

Dewey was interested in transforming occurrent interest into intrinsic interest or motivation. Yet for decades after Dewey's work, motivation was studied separately from learning or cognition; it is only recently that cognitive researchers have focused on motivation and its direct implication in thinking (Resnick and Klopfer, 1989, p. 7). Reconceptualizing motivation as internal instead of external has allowed us to move away from the more simplistic research on incentives and disincentives for workers and to think in more holistic terms that include challenging learning and meaningful social interactions in the workplace.

Several of these attributes or dispositions (such as innovation, curiosity, and motivation) are linked to the concept of creativity. Gardner (1963/1981) expanded the discussion of creativity to include receptivity and a freshness of perception, independence, flexibility, tolerance of ambiguity or uncertainty, a playfulness of ideas not bound by convention, and a capacity to find order or new patterns in experiences or ideas (pp. 32-40). Gardner's descriptors are echoed in Stone's (1987) conclusions about outstanding Teachers of the Year:

They share an extraordinary commitment to the teaching profession and its improvement. Individually, they are dedicated to the betterment of their students. They are highly creative and innovative in their methodology. They take pride in their work, viewing it as a personal signature. Each has a well-developed sense of humor and a balanced perspective on the world and his/her place in it. They genuinely love people and sincerely care about their needs. . . . Each has demonstrated that he/she has the ability to take any experience and turn it to his/her advantage. . . . They are empathetic, curious about everything. (pp. 136-137)

Many of the attributes of the self-renewing individual, as well as that of making increasingly good judgments, had earlier been described in Dewey's (1933/1960) explication of how we think. One might say that these attributes describe a lifelong learner or an educated person. The principles or dispositions of self-renewing individuals — to continually seek to learn, to commit to something they care about, to seek relationships with others, and to be innovative, flexible, and creative — are also noted consistently as characteristics of exemplary teachers. The same attributes appear again in the literature on teacher development and organizational climate.

Exemplary Teachers: A Neglected Resource in our Knowledge of Teacher Renewal

When the nominators of potential participants for this study were asked to describe their exemplary nominees, their comments included: innovative, continues to develop professionally, creative, flexible, caring, nurturing, child oriented, dedicated, positive, motivating, and excellent communicator. These descriptors parallel those generated by teachers in a focus group interview (part of an earlier pilot study I conducted) as well as in research on exemplary teachers (Easterly, 1983; Mertz, 1987; Penick, Yager, and Bonstetter, 1986; Shanoski and Hranitz, 1989; Stone, 1987; Van Schaack and Glick, 1982). They are seen as caring, creative, enthusiastic, and intellectually curious with positive attitudes about themselves and their students.

Van Schaack and Glick's (1982) "characteristics of superlative teachers" summarize well the existing research portrait of exemplary teachers:

1. a supportive family background;
2. a strong personal faith (not necessarily through organized religion);
3. enthusiasm for teaching;
4. self-confidence concerning their teaching;
5. excellent communicators;
6. socratic in their approach to teaching;
7. warmth (willing to give of themselves);
8. concern for students (genuine care);
9. avoidance of failure in students (see others' abilities and help them succeed);
10. a deep concern for professional development, a "commitment to renew themselves and improve their teaching." (pp. 31-33)

These researchers added that "superlative teachers are strong individuals; they have deep convictions and courage; they take risks" (p. 36).

The above descriptors of exemplary teachers seem to be broad and elusive, yet persons with such attributes have been known and recognizable for a long time. According to Jackson (1968/1990), "[a]lthough perfect agreement on who deserves the title [of exemplary teacher] may not exist, it is likely that in every school system there could be found at least a handful of teachers who would be called exemplary by almost any standard" (p. 115). Further, colleagues are capable of recognizing exemplary teachers (Ellett, Loup, Evans, and Chauvin, 1992; Stone, 1987; Van Schaack and Glick, 1982) and they consistently name three characteristics: **continuous learning; a care ethic** — concerns of care, nurturance of, and connectedness to others (Gilligan, 1982)**; and a commitment to teaching**. Campbell (1988) noted a "continual striving for personal growth that was inextricably tied to a sense of humaneness and tolerance" (p. 50) and concluded that the teachers' personal and professional worlds overlap in an integrated ethic.

Little else could be found in my literature search regarding exemplary teachers. Penick and associates (1986) reported that expert teachers of exemplary science programs have completed more years of graduate work than their colleagues and are active in professional organizations. Joyce and colleagues (1983) recognized that teachers who love learning (characterized as total omnivores) creatively seek out resources, colleagues, and improvement possibilities. In a study by Lieberman, Saxl, and Miles (1988), "master teachers" who became teacher leaders had been involved with writing and teaching new curriculum, had impressive backgrounds of academic accomplishments, had interpersonal skills, and were knowledgeable about schools, change, and organizations (p. 150).

Rewards for exemplary or "high-performing" teachers include student learning and student relationships, interaction with other high-performing teachers, challenge, autonomy, a sense of effectiveness (being able to use one's abilities), and meaningful adult feedback about classroom performance (Stevenson, 1986). In a study of career teachers, rewards such as opportunities for growth and interaction with respected colleagues (McLaughlin and Yee, 1988) are reminiscent of the psychic, intrinsic reward of "making a difference" (Lortie, 1975).

The above rewards are quite consistent with a grounded theory of adaptive strategies of experienced expert teachers (Campbell, 1988). These veteran exemplary teachers exhibited:

1. an intense belief in the importance of teaching;
2. a continuous search for ways to improve their professional growth;
3. a holistic view of teaching (their consummate reward being to play a part in seeing growth of students as whole human beings);
4. a high degree of personal and professional efficacy;
5. maintenance of a collegial support group holding a similar, positive outlook as well as a support group who validated their career choice;
6. a strong sense of professional autonomy;

7. a resistance against external factors perceived to interfere with their teaching mission. (pp. 62-71)

The themes of love of learning, a care ethic, and commitment to teaching are also alluded to in the literature on the improvement and professionalization of teachers (e.g., Holmes Group, 1986; 1990; Lieberman, 1988; Wasley, 1991) and, as noted in the literature on exemplary teachers, are associated with creativity, risk taking, and social interaction or collegiality. In other words, they seem to be highly desirable virtues and recognizable ideals of teachers.

Teacher Development

Professional growth, whether referred to as teacher development, professional development, or staff development, is generally understood in the literature to include the idea of improving teachers' and/or students' learning, or of deliberately changing teachers' beliefs (e.g., Fielding and Schalock, 1985; Griffin, 1983). Traditionally, it has often been referred to as "inservice education" and has not enjoyed a good reputation. Edelfelt and Lawrence (1975) echoed Lortie (1975) in concluding that teacher inservice education is piecemeal, patchwork, and haphazard; not receiving real commitment by either districts or universities; and seldom designed around teachers' needs. It has been noted for its episodic one-shot workshops, usually organized centrally with Little or no feedback or follow-up (Joyce and Showers, 1983; Leggett and Hoyle, 1987).

By 1980, both job-embedded growth and personal development for teachers were suggested as possibilities for improving professional growth (Yarger, Howey, and Joyce, 1980). However, Joyce and Showers (1988) noted recently that districts are still looking for ways to improve professional growth opportunities and to embed them in the worklife of teachers. It appears as though practice has not necessarily kept pace with research.

In the past decade, researchers contributed to the strengthening of both preservice and inservice education. A knowledge base on teaching was conceptualized (Reynolds, 1989) and there was an increased research focus on teaching and learning (e.g., Resnick and Klopfer, 1989) as well as on teachers' thought processes and actions, including differences between novice and expert teachers (e.g., Berliner, 1986; Clark and Peterson, 1986). Researchers also studied the effects of school cultures on teachers' learning and development (e.g., Feiman-Nemser and Floden, 1986) with emphasis on teachers' professional and practical knowledge (e.g., Tom and Valli, 1990), inquiry (e.g., Fosnot, 1989; Schon, 1987; Tikunoff and Mergendoller, 1983), and teacher leadership roles (e.g., Wasley, 1991).

An Expanded Definition of Professional Development
Howey's (1985) "expanded imperative" for professional development rested on six functions of staff development implicit in the professional literature. The six areas are not exclusive and, although the term "staff development" often connotes organizational renewal, I have argued above that individual and organizational renewal are two sides of the same coin. Indeed, Howey makes a point of including individual teacher development in the broader definition of staff development (p. 59). His expanded imperative includes continuing pedagogical development, understanding of self and others, cognitive development, theoretical development, professional development, and career development.

Pedagogical development
These activities focus on specific curriculum and instruction strategies or techniques and are usually presented in inservice training workshops. They tend to be "brief, atheoretical, and lacking in personal relationship to the life of teachers and their classrooms" (p. 58). In my teaching experience, this has been the dominant, almost exclusive kind of development offered by school districts and expected by teachers. Referred to within teaching as "how to" workshops, they are helpful in the sense of expanding the array of techniques or ideas in teachers' repertoires, especially for beginning teachers or teachers transferring to a new grade level.

Understanding of self and others
Howey presents numerous arguments for improving this area of development, chief among which is the importance and degree of human interaction in teaching. Lortie (1975) went so far as to suggest that teachers develop and use the self as a tool of the trade. This domain is highly developed in self-renewing individuals (Gardner, 1963/1981) and in teachers at high levels of psychological development and professional expertise (Heath, 1980; Leithwood, 1990). An understanding of self and others was evident in the teacher leaders studied by Lieberman, Saxl, and Miles (1988):

> These leaders were risktakers, willing to promote new ideas that might seem difficult or threatening to their colleagues. Their *interpersonal skills* — they knew how to be strong, yet caring and compassionate — helped them legitimate their positions in their schools amid often hostile and resistant staffs. (p. 150)

Mertz (1987), in his study of excellent teachers, wrote: "Self-knowledge, in effect, enables people to grow and to relate to other people in more productive, richer ways" (p. 30).

Cognitive development

As Howey (1985) points out, stage theorists such as Piaget (cognitive development), Kohlberg (moral), Loevinger (ego/self), Hunt (conceptual) and others argue that "human development, personality, and character are the results of changes in underlying cognitive and emotional structure" (p. 60). This has implications for teachers: ability for imagining alternative possibilities or multiple perspectives, formulating hypotheses, reflection, judgment, flexibility, and interpersonal sensitivity (p. 60). As mentioned earlier, these dispositions are included in Gardner's principles of self-renewal and reflect a recognizable intellectual posture (e.g., Dewey, 1933/1960; Jackson, 1987). Heath (1980) contends that these dispositions support teacher certainty in that they allow teachers to trust their ability to solve problems.

Cognitive development of teachers would allow teachers to "develop a capacity for effecting renewal and establish mechanisms for doing this" (Goodlad, 1984).

> Existing processes involving the identification of problems, the gathering of relevant data, the formulation of solutions, and the monitoring of actions take care of both business as usual and change. This is the self-renewing capability school personnel must develop if their place of work is to be productive and satisfying. (p. 276)

Theoretical development

At the turn of the century, Dewey (1904/1965) made a plea as well as an argument for teachers to balance theory and practice in a systematic inquiry of their daily work. Howey (1985) essentially makes the same argument: Teachers do not have a tradition of articulating and examining the personal or formal theories that drive their practice. This would call for reflection, experimentation with alternatives, analysis, and theory development. Ideally, the result would be more rational and coherent practice to enhance student learning as well as to encourage a deeper understanding of practice, theory, and research (also see Ross, Cornett, and McCutcheon, 1992).

In the discussion about schools as communities of learning for teachers and students (e.g., Sarason, 1990; Talbert, 1993), the assumption is that one way of reducing the theory/practice gap would be for teachers to examine and articulate their own practice and practical knowledge and to seek evidence in order to make defensible judgments. Kaestle (1993) elaborates the problem of ignoring the practical knowledge of teachers and the complex variables they deal with: "Not only does it misconceive research, but it impoverishes our view of practice as divorced from fundamental inquiry. The two must be merged, supporting work on practical problems in classroom settings because it will also yield fundamental insights into the learning process" (p. 26).

Professional development

Drawing on the literature on professionalization of teachers, Howey (1985) argues that teachers, unlike other professionals, are not characterized by their ability to make informed judgments grounded in specialized knowledge. They rarely contribute to the professional research in education (p. 61). Little (1987) takes the same position:

> Responsibility for accumulating, evaluating, and disseminating knowledge about teaching and learning has not been vested in teachers. Teachers have few mechanisms for adding to the knowledge base in teaching and leave no legacy of insights, methods, and materials at the close of a long career. . . . No one is evaluated, either positively or negatively, on the basis of contributions they have made to the knowledge base of the profession or to the teaching proficiency of others. (p. 502-503)

Because of this and because of misconceptions or erroneous interpretations of research by teachers, Howey (1985) calls for better producers and consumers of research. Systematic inquiry or collaborative research and development by teachers could be enriching to the profession and valuable professional development for teachers (p. 61).

Career development

What is proposed here is staff development activities designed to address differentiated leadership roles for teachers, roles such as peer coach, mentor, team leader, resource teacher, and other similar positions. "Training should include inquiry into what is known about how teachers learn and develop, inquiry into how schools and classrooms affect the learning and development of teachers, and inquiry into what is known about the organization, management, and delivery of inservice teacher education" (Howey, 1985, p. 62).

Recent Trends in Teacher Development

Particularly in the last decade, professional development has expanded to include job-embedded professional growth activities that teachers can engage in alone or in small groups, largely in the course of their on-going instructional activities. Essentially, these activities are undertaken *by* teachers *for* teachers and have as key goals: improving practice to help children learn, linking preservice and inservice development, renewing veteran teachers, and promoting continuous growth and learning.

Examples include inquiry (e.g., Short, 1991; Tikunoff and Mergendoller, 1983), action research (e.g., Grundy), teacher reflection (e.g., Schon, 1987), mentoring (e.g., Little, 1990), peer coaching (Joyce and Showers, 1980), and increasingly, teacher reasoning and decision making (e.g., McNergney, Lloyd, Mintz, and Moore, 1988; Rental, 1992; Simmons and Schuette, 1988). Other examples for teacher renewal include teacher leadership roles (e.g., Wasley, 1991), clinical faculty positions in Professional Development Schools (Holmes Group, 1990), and the North Carolina Center for the Advancement of Teaching (Rud and Oldendorf, 1992). These possibilities offer teachers opportunities for growth and learning as well as collegial interaction: teacher development as a process rather than a series of unconnected events.

However, Fullan and Hargreaves (1992) underscore the work that remains to be done in the area of teacher development:

> The teacher as a person has also been neglected in teacher development. Most approaches to staff development, for example, either treat all teachers as if they are the same (or should be the same), or stereotype teachers as innovators, resisters, and the like. In more recent research, we are seeing that age, stage of career, life experiences, and gender factors — things that make up the total person — affect people's interest in and response to innovation and their motivation to seek improvement. . . . And most approaches still fail to value (and consequently fail to involve) the veteran teacher. (p. 5)

Teachers' Biographies

As researchers learn more about teacher development, there appears to be a shift toward the Holistic Orientation of professional development, a perspective that focusses on the individual as actively seeking meaning and where all aspects of development (cognitive, physical, social, emotional) are considered as a whole (Holly, 1983). Holly (1983) believes that an environment that is informal, open, encouraging of experimentation and play, and a challenge to creative capacities is necessary for adults' growth, although climate does not guarantee growth.

Some attention is being given to personal dimensions of teachers' lives and professional growth (e.g., Ball and Goodson, 1985; Bolin and Falk, 1987; Goodson, 1992; Mertz, 1987). Although it seems logical to think that the experiences throughout the many years before a teacher goes to college have shaped that individual in multiple ways, life before preservice is rarely considered. What Campbell (1990-91) concluded from his study on expert teachers, though, was that factors such as "a holistic view of teaching, personal and professional efficacy, and selection of a peer support group may be amenable to developmental strategies in preservice and inservice education programs [but] seem to hinge upon what potential teachers bring to education programs and school districts" (p. 39).

Nevertheless, in stage or life cycle theories of teachers, there still seems to be a desire to separate individuals' experiences prior to becoming a teacher from their professional or career life (see Christensen, 1985 for a brief review of career stage development). Huberman (1989) extends the debate by delving more deeply into possible development variations, especially of veteran teachers, but warns that such stages are suspect because they are unlikely to describe single individuals and are simply a construct to help us keep order in our minds until we can handle more complexity (p. 53).

Teachers as Adult Learners

In the area of adult learning, we know that adult learners should set their own goals (Kidd, 1976) and that choices and individualized development are preferable (Krupp, 1981) since adults are more receptive to learning if it can be applied directly to their personal professional life (Knowles, 1978). In a review of the literature on adult learning, Bryant (1981) wrote that if adults "require learning that is self-paced, self-directed, relevant to personal or career interests and participatory in nature . . . . [a] process design is favored over a content design" (p. 60). "Addressing the needs of teachers as learners throughout the [inservice] program promotes a safe climate in which teachers can take risks" (Valencia and Killion, 1988). "There should be an open, trusting atmosphere where mistakes are viewed as opportunities for learning" (Holly, 1983, p. 23).

Adults, depending on education and experience (not on their age), are at various levels of psychological, moral, and conceptual development (Thies-Sprinthall and Sprinthall, 1987). This area of research may provide us with a deeper and more adequate understanding of exemplary experienced teachers. Sprinthall and Thies-Sprinthall (1983) make several claims as a result of their cognitive-developmental research:

1. Growth is neither automatic nor unilateral but occurs only with appropriate interaction between the human and the environment.
2. ". . . [W]e can make the general claim that adults at more complex stage levels [of cognitive and moral development] function in more humane and democratic modes than those at less complex stages." In a study of physicians, this was true regardless of academic achievement (p. 18).
3. ". . . [P]ersons judged at higher stages of development function more complexly, possess a wider repertoire of behavioral skills, perceive problems more broadly, and can respond more accurately and empathically to the needs of others" (p. 21).

Their research suggests that fruitful relations with other people (Gardner, 1963/ 1981) and a strong care ethic, noted in self-renewing individuals and exemplary teachers, are linked to the cognitive realm.

Leithwood (1990) synthesized some of the existing research to describe teachers at a high level of psychological and professional development. A teacher candidate at the highest stage of psychological development:

- has already learned to appreciate multiple possibilities, multiple perspectives, and interdependency of relationships;
- is future oriented;
- is capable of synthesis (not only of perspectives, but also of a balanced achievement/interpersonal emphasis in the classroom);
- understands the reasons for rules, the need for exceptions, and the ways they as individuals cope with the resulting conflicts;
- controls the classroom in collaboration with the students and encourages complex functioning and learning, creativity and flexibility.

A teacher at the highest levels of professional expertise:

- is reflective and understands the assumptions, beliefs, and values behind choices;
- is capable of assisting colleagues informally and formally, first inside the school and then across the system;
- is well informed about district policies and procedures;
- is committed to educational improvement. (pp. 74-78)

Adding empirical results from cognitive developmental theory, the professional teacher exhibits empathy, flexibility, and high levels of humane and democratic values (Sprinthall and Thies-Sprinthall, 1983). Taken together, they reflect most of Gardner's principles and certainly the three major characteristics of exemplary teachers: continuous learning, care, and commitment.

The question, then, is how to design teacher education in ways that will assist the renewal of teachers throughout their career. Houle (cited in Willie and Howey, 1980) identified four areas important to those concerned with self-renewal:

1. keeping up with professional knowledge;
2. mastering new conceptions within their profession;
3. continuing to study disciplines supporting their profession;
4. growing as persons as well as professionals.

Willie and Howey (1980) expanded these dimensions to include "the need to understand the interaction of physiological, psychological, and social aspects in human development and the impact of that interaction upon one's self and the people one serves" (p. 27). They believe that "[t]he ability to experience open, supportive even tender relationships not only with students but also with colleagues . . . is essential to good teaching" (p. 38) and suspect that "reciprocity, self-disclosure, and mutual respect are essential ingredients in most authentic forms of teaching and learning" (p. 38).

Heath (1980), in discussing psychological maturity of teachers, also contends that teachers who have a deep understanding of self and others, who "can create collaborative working relationships with other teachers and their students will create more adaptive ways of teaching tomorrow" (p. 297). Heath notes that such teachers "can analyze objectively, accurately understand, care for, and respect the diversity of their students" (p. 297). They test out hypotheses about teaching and eventually, repeating approaches that worked, develop some habitual, stable ways of approaching teaching. It is this that allows effective teachers "to maintain their intellectual efficiency when despairing or upset" (p. 297).

As we have seen, renewal is a complex concept that is interrelated with many other concepts such as creativity, self-knowledge, relationships, commitment, values, caring, growth, and risk taking. The literature on organizational climate is instructive in elaborating the connections between self-renewing individuals and organizations.

Organizational Climate

Within the body of literature on organizational climate, the Quality of Work Life (QWL) interpretation focusses on the micro-organizational environments of schools; that is, restructuring and enhancing teachers' daily experiences (Louis and Smith, 1990). It emphasizes individual satisfaction as well as the promotion of effectiveness of performance; in this, it is different from but "more useful than professional models . . . which are theoretically detached from individual performance issues" (p. 34). The dimensions of QWL representing social-psychological perceptions of the workplace include:

1. respect from relevant adults (see Louis, 1992 for teachers equating respect with trust and the priority they put on being respected by colleagues);
2. genuine opportunities for participation in decision making (Kanter, 1981 noted that this and the opportunity to engage in collaborative professional activities are powerful intrinsic rewards);

3. frequent and stimulating professional interaction with peers which encourages substantially more innovations (supported by Little, 1982);
4. a high sense of efficacy;
5. opportunity to use and develop skills and knowledge;
6. sufficient resources to support teacher experimentation;
7. reasonable congruence between teachers' personal goals (usually cognitive, personal, and social development for students) and the goals of the school in general (colleagues, including the administrator). (pp. 35-37)

In the schools that Louis and Smith (1990) studied, the teachers "felt professional" and felt they were "treated like a professional;" the schools emphasized and supported professional development; the schools offered expanded teacher roles; innovations were encouraged and it was considered "o.k. to fail, but important to try" (p. 38); team teaching was common; peer observation and feedback on performance was frequent; and several of the schools held retreats or social activities to encourage collegiality (pp. 37-39).

These findings underscore what had been suspected for some time: that "we have seriously oversimplified what motivates people toward participation and underrated the complexity of the contexts within which school people work" (Lieberman and Rosenholtz, 1987, p. 89). The results also parallel Goodlad's observation (cited in Stoll, 1992): "that successful school improvement can only result if the environment is one in which the collaborative study of teaching occurs, and risk-taking is encouraged in an atmosphere of trust and support . . . . such that teachers are able to work together to examine their behavior, secure in the knowledge that they can take risks and that they are a part of a mutual support system" (p. 118).

Following a period where researchers attached almost naive negativism to teacher isolation and optimism to teacher collaboration, some realized that there are gaps in our understanding of individualism, individuality, collaboration, and collegiality (e.g., Hargreaves, 1993; Little, 1992a). Many dimensions of teachers' independence and collegiality, especially colleagueship beyond the school walls, have not been examined in a way that allows for more robust conceptualization (Little, 1992a).

Trust and support may be an important link between the image of "being a teacher" (Little, 1992a) and the wider context of the professional community. That trust (equated with respect and being treated like a professional) is mentioned so often seems more than coincidental. Heath (1980) posited that trust is one of four principles that contribute to allocentric maturation (the ability to understand a multiplicity of perspectives). Since this ability is compatible with the dispositions of a self-renewing individual, it appears reasonable that the maturing individual would seek relationships and conditions that foster further growth. The resulting colleagueship may, however, be balanced with being a teacher in the sense of needing to spend time with students to ensure learning and see growth (see Hargreaves, 1993).

Teachers' Workplace

It was Rosenholtz (1989) who made the connection between the structures and processes influencing schools and how they appear to the teachers who work in them. Concerned with the narrow definition of school success (student achievement) and the lack of theoretical support underpinning the huge literature on effective schools, Rosenholtz sought to explain how schools affect teachers' beliefs, cognitions, and behaviors and how those teachers' beliefs, cognitions, and behaviors reciprocally affect schools. She described how facilitating or inhibiting school climates affect the lives of teachers and the quality of teaching and learning within various cultures. She outlined the conditions that produce "learning enriched" or "learning impoverished" environments; conditions such as relationships with students and other adults, and normative beliefs about learning and teaching. She argued that there are shared aspects of work that cut across, and are more powerful than, individual biographies teachers bring to the workplace (p. 4). Those aspects include shared goals, collaboration, teacher certainty, and teacher commitment.

Shared goals

Ambiguous goals encourage norms of self-reliance and professional isolation. However, when teaching is acknowledged to be difficult and complex, teachers realize that even their most capable peers are challenged and need help, but that seeking it does not diminish their worth as an individual. "[T]he less ego-endangering teachers' workplace circumstances, the more they will request and offer advice and assistance to accomplish agreed-upon goals" (p. 6).

Collaboration

The second aspect deals with collaboration among individuals in a school. In "moving" schools (as compared with "stuck" schools), resources and personnel were marshalled to enable teachers to request and offer assistance in helping colleagues to improve. This openness represented a tacit or explicit acknowledgement that teaching is complex and that colleagues are valuable sources of knowledge and support. A collaborative culture in moving schools was closely related to learning for both students and teachers. "[S]hared goals confer legitimacy, support, and pressure not to deviate from norms of school renewal . . . [and] the greater teachers' opportunities for learning, the more their students tend to learn" (p. 7). "Overwhelmingly, the teachers who proved most consistently enthusiastic about professional development were also those who worked in schools that made both formal and informal learning an integral part of teachers' work" (Little, 1992b, p. 180).

Teacher certainty

Teachers who want to learn, who want to become more skilled and more knowledgeable, will confront new challenges and take risks. Teacher certainty about their instructional practices allows teachers to try innovations. Each success (increased student learning) then strengthens teachers' beliefs that children can learn and leads to greater effort by the teachers (also see Little, 1982). Each success reinforces teacher certainty and increases the possibility that they will again undertake innovation, along with its inherent risks.

Uncertain teachers tend to blame teaching success and failure on external causes over which they have no control (students' ability, parents, disadvantaged environments, etc.). These teachers do not risk challenges, they lower their expectations of and involvement with students, and they have higher absentee rates (Rosenholtz, 1989, pp. 142-143). Rosenholtz describes their work as "routine" instead of the "nonroutine" work that teachers in learning enriched schools engage in. Routine work does not encourage growth; as such, it represents an ecology of stability in which renewal cannot occur. The explanation, according to Dewey (1933/1960), depends on thinking, without which learning does not occur: Thinking is what allows us to move away from routine activity, to plan, to act with intention, to understand consequences, to enrich things with meaning, to invent, to value and make judgments (pp. 16-21).

Teacher commitment

"The absence of conditions for high internal motivation has profound and deleterious consequences for people's workplace commitment" (Rosenholtz, 1989, p. 143) including a diminishing esteem derived from their work, a focus on social rather than professional relationships with colleagues, and little future planning. Important conditions for commitment include "learning opportunities, opportunities to increase one's talents and instructional strategies to better master one's environment, to repel professional stagnation, and to experience a sense of continuous progress and growth" (p. 164). Growth, then, acts as a reward in itself as well as a stimulus for further renewal and challenge. This increases teachers' certainty, psychic rewards (e.g., relationships with students), discretion and control of the terms of work, and commitment to their work (p. 144).

Learning and Efficacy

There is a great deal of conceptual ambiguity and inconsistency concerning teacher efficacy. However, it is broadly understood as teachers' belief in their ability to influence students' learning or to make a difference. The latter is often mentioned by teachers and refers to the powerful psychic rewards of caring for children and seeing them learn (Lortie, 1975). Efficacy is also "presumed to be a relatively predispositional state" (Smylie, 1990, p. 57). The definition Rosenholtz (1989) employs is linked to the construct of teacher certainty grounded in knowledge of their practice: awareness of their practices or behaviors, and the intended outcomes for or effect on students' learning.

Experienced exemplary teachers were found to have a high degree of personal and professional efficacy (Campbell, 1988). Compared to teachers with a low sense of efficacy, teachers with a high sense of efficacy communicate high expectations to students, persist longer in helping students to be successful, and are more tolerant of students' failures (Gibson and Dembo, 1984). They also communicate the importance of learning to students, take a personal interest in what students do, establish warm relationships with students (Ashton and Webb, 1986), and have a positive effect on students' academic achievement (Rosenholtz, 1989; Smylie, 1990). Positive links have also been made between teachers' high sense of efficacy and classroom innovations or change (McLaughlin and Marsh, 1978; Smylie, 1990), their participation in collegial collaboration and decision making (Ashton and Webb, 1986; McLaughlin and Marsh, 1978), and their willingness to involve parents in the school (Rosenholtz, 1989).

Smylie (1990) underlines the difficulty of researching and interpreting data in the area of efficacy because of the variations in definition and the complexity of teachers' work and workplace. However, given Rosenholtz's definition (see above), Smylie (1990) argues that promoting efficacy through encouraging teachers' knowledge of self, knowledge of classroom practices, and examination of the outcomes of practices may be internally motivating and may cause dynamic disequilibrium (Joyce, 1984) leading to alteration of and improvement in teaching practice. This argument supports the call for cognitive development, theoretical development, and an understanding of self outlined by Howey (1985). Both lines of thought would require that teachers be learners and that such development be part of teacher education.

Commitment

Commitment is also a term appearing frequently in the literature on organizational climate. It seems to be associated with career choice, retention or attrition of teachers, and teacher attitudes toward job satisfaction and performance (Kottkamp, 1990; Reyes, 1990) even though the assumptions and causal relationships between satisfaction and performance are in doubt and there is little understanding of the attitudes involved (Kottkamp, 1990).

Rosenholtz (1989) argues that several conditions are necessary to sustain teachers' commitment to the workplace.

These factors include psychic rewards, where teachers are acknowledged for their special competencies and worth; task autonomy and discretion, where teachers control the terms of work and are therefore able to assess their unique contributions to it; learning opportunities that provide an ongoing challenge and a sense of personal accomplishment; and teacher certainty, which lends the confidence needed to approach new work challenges. (p. 144)

A recent theoretical model of teacher commitment (Reyes, 1990) indicates that committed teachers work harder and perform their job better than uncommitted teachers, are less inclined to leave teaching, are more likely to devote time to extracurricular activities, and are more likely to see increases in student achievement and positive affective characteristics.

What else might shed light on why some teachers are committed and others are not? Recent research gives us an idea of the organizational climate that fosters commitment although to date, the literature on commitment does not take into consideration the possibility of individual dispositions or teachers' experiences prior to becoming a committed teacher. Nor does it consider differing levels of commitment or the fragility of commitment (an exception is Yee, 1990 who mentions the latter).

Rosenholtz (1989) suggests that one viable strategy for improving the learning of some teachers is for practitioners to become researchers in their own setting, "enlarging their own capacity to identify problems and collect and interpret data. . . . not only to teach in one's classroom, but to learn to enhance one's craft on a continuous basis, to inquire into problems of pedagogy, and to organize for and facilitate the professional development of one's peers" (p. 220). If commitment is seen as similar to Gardner's (1963/1981) conceptualization of motivation (doing something about which one cares deeply), then school cultures that build and sustain personal relationships, that encourage learning opportunities, and that value teachers and students as learners should be motivating and compatible places for self-renewing teachers to work.

Collaboration and Collegiality

The literature discussed so far has described various different kinds of human interactions: between teachers and students, teachers and parents, teachers and colleagues. Hoy, Tarter, and Kottkamp (1991) constructed a heuristic description of a healthy school around teacher/colleague relationships. Within the last decade, following the ground-breaking study by Little (1982), there has been an increasing amount of attention to teacher/colleague interactions, often loosely referred to as collaboration or collegiality.

Collegiality is in stark contrast to the literature which is replete with studies stating that teachers work in isolation (Goodlad, 1984; Lieberman, Saxl, and Miles, 1988; Lortie, 1975; Wasley, 1991) within the "cell"-like structures of so many schools

(Goodlad, 1984). Lieberman and Rosenholtz (1987) described how isolation is a barrier to innovation and growth:

> Years of imposed innovations — to be implemented every September 1st — have taught teachers that they will not be involved in decisions of how or why a new innovation is to be adopted and will not be given assistance, support, or time to implement it, whatever the idea. Most school people have learned to rely solely on themselves and their own experimental learning. What they learn is idiosyncratic. Isolation and insulation are the expected conditions in too many schools. These conditions do not foster individual teacher growth and school improvement. (p. 94)

The differences and contradictions between individual and collective needs of teachers quickly became excessive extremes: collaboration as an antidote for isolation; community versus individualism; professional autonomy versus individual autonomy. The last decade has "witnessed a virtual campaign to break the bounds of privacy in teaching. It is a campaign waged less often by teachers themselves than by those who would reform their work and workplaces" (Little and McLaughlin, 1993, p. 1). This occurred despite Little understanding of collegiality or collaboration and continues despite the knowledge that "contrived collegiality" does not work (Grimmett and Crehan, 1992; Hargreaves and Dawe, 1990). We also know that surface collegiality may actually subvert good practice and conceptions of professionalism; for example, members of a school culture or subculture may be collegial but reinforce spending minimal time and energy on teaching (Little and McLaughlin, 1993).

> [Such interactions] underscore the limitations of theoretical and empirical work devoted primarily to collegial forms and processes that give comparatively superficial attention to the content expressed: the beliefs that teachers hold singly and collectively about children and learning and the professional expertise that teachers admire (or do not admire) in their own and others' teaching. (p. 5)

Additionally, we know that there are differing degrees of collegiality (Little, 1989):

> "Weak" and "strong" versions of collegial relations plausibly produce or sustain quite different conditions of teacher performance and commitment. Patterns of interaction that support mutual assistance or routine sharing may account well for maintaining a certain level of workforce stability, teacher

satisfaction, and a performance "floor"; they seem less likely, however, to account for high rates of innovation or for high levels of collective commitment to specific curricular or instructional policies. They seem less likely to force teachers' collective confrontation with the school's fundamental purposes or with the implications of the pattern or practices that have accumulated over time. (p. 30)

The greater the isolation of teachers, the lower their teaching skills were found to be (Rosenholtz and Smylie, 1984). The studies on teacher isolation appear to limit teacher interactions to the walls of their classrooms or schools. Studies of exemplary teachers, however, show that their definition of teaching and learning is much broader than this: "They [exemplary teachers] don't see their classroom as their only teaching area. They have a more global attitude" (Mertz, 1987, p. 22). In observations of outstanding teachers, Wigginton (1985) noticed that "they build relationships among their peers, fighting isolation with as much strength as they can muster, knowing that such networks are their life-support systems as well as their sources for new ideas and input. . . . They tend to be involved in the community . . . in ways other than teaching . . . [and] have numerous friendships outside the teaching profession" (pp. 283-284). Stevenson (1986) and Campbell (1988) commented that interactions were so crucial to the level of work and satisfaction of high-performing teachers that they deliberately sought out other good teachers inside and outside their school buildings.

In discussing teacher-student realationships, Hargreaves (1993) suggests that what has been called teacher isolation may really reflect an ethic of care rather than the negative overtones it so often carries. If psychic rewards — caring for children and being rewarded by seeing them learn — are so important to committed teachers, it is logical that they would want to spend time interacting with students as well as adults. In Hargreaves' study, teachers felt that increased preparation time for collaborative planning with other teachers took them away from teaching and being with their students. They also worried that collaboration would demand sameness instead of encouraging teacher creativity and innovation which they desired. But paradoxically, they enjoyed collegial interaction because it too has the potential for exploring ideas and spurring creativity. This suggests that there may be a complex balance of relationships (teachers and students, teachers and colleagues) and differently weighted reasons for interactions that are not yet understood.

Hargreaves (1993) notes that being trusted with discretionary judgment (creativity in curriculum presentation, in this case) was an important component of teacher competence and effectiveness (efficacy). Rosenholtz (1989) associated discretionary judgment (task autonomy) with commitment (p. 141) and nonroutinization (p. 194), but not with efficacy. It seems possible that task autonomy is also motivated by a care ethic: the desire to search for ways of teaching that will help children learn, thereby providing psychic rewards for the teacher. It may be an alternative understanding of innovation: "creative persons . . . have faith in their capacity to do the things they want and need to do in the area of their chosen work" (Gardner, 1963/1981, p. 39).

The attributes of learning, care, and collaboration seem to be intertwined in complex ways not yet understood. Teachers appear to require solitude for long-term planning, creativity, and reflection (Hargreaves, 1993) balanced with social interaction for varying reasons and at different levels of intimacy with students, colleagues, parents, and others in the workplace or beyond. Teachers report deep enjoyment from being with students as well as from the stimulation of being with respected colleagues (Joyce and Showers, 1988; Louis, 1992; McLaughlin and Yee, 1988).

Conclusion

If we want self-renewing teachers, we need to understand their characteristics and then seek and support environments that encourage the pursuit of those ideals. Although many researchers have tried in many ways to understand the complexity of exemplary, self-renewing teachers and the environments that sustain the dispositions they exhibit, none has made the associations as interconnected and explicit as Gardner (1963/1981). Argued from many perspectives, the call for teachers as learners seems to have top priority: Self-renewal of individuals and organizations depends on learning as a lifelong habit. "The formation of habits is a purely mechanical thing unless habits are also *tastes* — habitual modes of preference and esteem, an effective sense of excellence" (Dewey, 1916/1966, p. 102).

What also appears in the literature on exemplary teachers is the overwhelming importance of human interactions in order for learning to occur (also see Dewey, 1938; Vygotsky, 1978). Although there have been many calls for mentoring, peer coaching, team teaching, and the like, they tend to be proffered as ways of "professionalizing" teaching, not as necessary means for learning.

Our understanding of dispositions (habits of good thinking) that self-renewing teachers have learned is also far from complete. That those attributes are desirable for all teachers is evident in the literature. But Gardner (1963/1981) warns that ". . . a strong tradition of freedom of thought and inquiry is essential to continuous renewal" (p. 33). Societies or organizations are renewed "by people who believe in something, care about something, stand for something" (p. 115). Self-renewing teachers must have a vision of something worth saving. Yet, if Gardner is correct, there cannot be long-term, continuous renewal without liberty (the disciplining of power and the dispersal of power), regard for the worth of the individual, and pluralism (many decision points rather than only one, a willingness to entertain diverse views, access to multiple ways of knowing and expressing views) (pp. xv; 67). It may be that the most fruitful research will result from an exploration of how self-renewing teachers began to develop their dispositions and an examination of whether the schools that enable them to renew are rooted in, and strive to practice, democratic ideals.

Summary

This chapter reviewed Gardner's (1963/1981) conceptualization of self-renewal and related literature on exemplary teachers, teacher development, and organizational climate. Three characteristics of exemplary teachers were highlighted throughout: continuous learning, an ethic of care, and commitment. Chapter 3 will describe the methodology of this study.

CHAPTER III
METHODOLOGY

Put briefly, the issue is to develop a modality of educational research which speaks both within and to the teacher.

Goodson (1992, p. 15)

The characteristics of self-renewing individuals (Gardner, 1963/1981), effects of organizational climate on teachers' renewal (Rosenholtz, 1989), and an expanded definition of teacher development (Howey, 1985) provided a conceptual framework for examining the complex realm of teacher renewal and interpreting the data. The goal of the study was not to generate theory, but to understand the process (as well as the outcomes) of renewal for exemplary veteran teachers in an urban setting and their perceptions of the significance of personal and organizational factors affecting their renewal.

Rationale for Qualitative Research

Teachers' perceptions of personal and professional self-renewal imply complex reasoning, relationships, and behavior. Understanding the process of renewal and the participants' interpretation of their thoughts, feelings, and actions requires a research framework that permits the inquirer and participants to delve "in depth into complexities and processes" (Marshall and Rossman, 1989, p. 46). It should also allow the researcher to tease out thoughts and subtleties that might remain unarticulated without human interaction. The meaning and shape of the study depend heavily on "the interaction between [the] investigator and context. . . [T]he nature of mutual shapings cannot be known until they are witnessed" (Lincoln and Guba, 1985, p. 208). Further, "qualitative researchers assume that human behavior is significantly influenced by the setting in which it occurs" (Bogdan and Biklen,

1992, p. 30). In other words, teachers live in an indeterminate and unpredictable setting that influences their perceptions and requires a correspondingly flexible research design as relevant variables and patterns surface throughout the course of the study.

The study relied on in-depth interviews as the primary method of data collection. Participants were asked to reflect on past experiences and to reconstruct events and lines of reasoning. Lincoln and Guba (1985) contend that qualitative research allows the inquirer, as the research instrument, to adapt to the situation, to see a holistic context, to cope with complexity, to ask for amplification or clarification, and to explore anomalies (pp. 193-194).

This study also required an interpretive paradigm since conclusions are grounded in the contexts of the teachers' lives rather than in existing theory. The purpose of the research was to explore how exemplary veteran teachers self-renew personally and professionally and to understand the influence of organizational factors that enabled and/or constrained their renewal.

The Case Study Method

The case study method has become a mainstay of educational research (Merriam, 1988) particularly since it allows the researcher to explore and describe the perceptions of individuals or a group when the context, setting, or frame of reference is important (Marshall and Rossman, 1989, p. 46). "A *case* refers both to an event or happening and to the actions and experiences of a person or a collectivity" (Denzin, 1989, p. 185).

The case study is not a technique, but a way of organizing social data (Goode and Hatt, 1952, p. 331). It allows the researcher to understand the uniqueness or idiosyncracy of a case in its complexity without necessarily seeking what is common or generalizable (Stake, 1988, p. 256). Stake (1978) argues that case studies are often "the preferred method of research [social inquiry] because they may be epistemologically in harmony with the reader's experience and thus to that person a natural basis for generalization" (p. 5). He describes case studies as follows:

> In the social science literature, most case studies feature descriptions that are complex, holistic, and involving a myriad of not highly isolated variables . . . . Themes and hypotheses may be important, but they remain subordinate to the understanding of the case. Although case studies have been used . . . as a method of exploration preliminary to theory development, the characteristics of the method are usually more suited to expansionist than reductionist pursuits. . . . Its best use appears to me to be for adding to existing experience and humanistic understanding. (p. 7)

The Researcher's Role

Qualitative researchers are aware of the dangers of subjectivity, of "going native," and of analyzing subjective data. However, as Goetz and LeCompte (1981) point out, "The goal is to reconstruct the categories used by subjects to conceptualize their own experiences and world view" (p. 54). As a veteran, female, urban elementary school teacher myself, I risk criticism that being an "insider" can make the ordinary so familiar that important data are overlooked or left unexplained (Fetterman, 1989; Jackson, 1968/1990). However, as Cheater (cited in Peshkin, 1988) has pointed out, "We cannot rid ourselves of this subjectivity, nor should we wish to; but we ought, perhaps, to pay it very much more attention" (p. 17). By being aware of what I see and don't see, I do not "exorcise my subjectivity. I do, rather, enable myself to manage it . . . . [and] consciously attend to the orientations that will shape what I see and what I make of what I see" (Peshkin, 1988, pp. 20-21). In this study, member checks, peer debriefers, and my advisory committee helped act as safeguards against my subjectivity.

There are, however, advantages to being an insider if prudence and good judgment are exercised. Calderhead (cited in Clark and Peterson, 1986) noted that experienced teachers (insiders) extracted more and deeper meaning than beginning teachers (outsiders) were capable of gleaning in schools. There was a marked difference in the nature, level, and sophistication of their interpretations and understanding of classroom events compared to those of novices (p. 279). During the interviews, I was aware that not only my teaching experience, but also my supervision of preservice and inservice teachers, helped me to hone in on specifics and innuendoes and elicit more thoughtful or elaborated responses from the teacher participants than first proffered.

I was also aware of teacher statements that were subtle insider talk that only another experienced teacher would discern (Miles and Huberman, 1984, p. 48). For example, one participant explained that when she was transferred to a new school early in her career, she was assigned to the library learning center. I understood the transfer-by-low-seniority system and the longstanding tradition of placing new teachers in open space areas like library learning centers. In the seventies (at the time of her transfer), such areas were considered an "architectural fad" and were generally avoided by veteran teachers.

As a naturalistic researcher, I had to encourage openness and avoid the appearance of judgment. Accomplishing this required "empathic neutrality": that is, "[t]he neutral investigator enters the research arena with no axe to grind, no theory to prove, and no predetermined results to support" (Patton, 1990, pp. 54-55). Teacher or not, my depth of participation depended on constant renegotiation of entry, trust, and understanding throughout the research project (Wax, 1971, pp. 46-47). I was aware of the warning that researchers may presume to "be the guardian of rationality, efficiency, and morality" (Stake, 1988, p. 272) and there were times when I had to consciously set aside judgment in an attempt to understand a participant's choices and decisions in a given situation. For example, my initial reaction to one participant's view of motherhood was negative until I discovered her ethnic and religious background. These teachers willingly opened their lives to examination, making themselves vulnerable in the process, and so, like Noffke (1990) and McLaren (1991, p. 154), I wanted to "collaborate *with*" the participants instead of "doing research *on*" them.

The level of trust and engagement on the part of the participants may, in part, be judged by the following situations that occurred during or after the data collection period:

1. Without any solicitation, the participants offered or showed me resumés; photos of a major curriculum innovation; favorite professional books; a childhood composition, "When I grow up, I want to be a teacher;" and a video clip of an interview made by a local television station to honor one of the participants as an outstanding teacher.
2. A week after the final interview, one participant phoned me to say she had thought more deeply about one of the questions and wanted to elaborate a response she had given during the interview.
3. One participant wrote a note of thanks "for the soul searching moments" the interviews had prompted. Another participant waited until I had turned off the tape recorder to discuss her indecision concerning a new position she had been offered and then wrote: "I really appreciate all of your support during my decision making process and the reading material you let me borrow. I am so glad I have had the opportunity to get to know you." Both of these teachers have since asked me for further information and materials to assist them in curriculum leadership roles within their district.

Data Collection

Selection of Participants

One of the major objectives of this study was to examine how teachers nominated as exemplary self-renew. A pilot study I had conducted earlier and my review of the literature confirmed what Jackson (1968/1990) had predicted: that "[a]lthough perfect agreement on who deserves the title [of exemplary teacher] may not exist, it is likely that in every school system there could be found at least a handful of teachers who would be called exemplary by almost any standard" (p. 115). The pilot study included observation in the classroom of an urban teacher nominated as outstanding; an unstructured interview to determine her understanding of exemplary teacher; and a focus group interview with educators in a different urban district to elaborate their perceptions of an exemplary teacher.

Ellett, Loup, Evans, and Chauvin (1992), investigating the validity of teacher nominations of "superior" colleagues through comprehensive classroom-based assessments of teaching and learning, found that teachers could consistently and accurately identify exemplary peers. An earlier but smaller study also found peer nomination of exemplary teachers to be accurate and reliable (Van Schaack and Glick, 1982).

When I compared the qualities and descriptions of exemplary teachers by the educators who participated in my pilot study with similar research on characteristics of outstanding or superlative teachers (Easterly, 1983; Shanoski and Hranitz, 1989; Van Schaack and Glick, 1982), a consistent portrait or understanding of exemplary teachers emerged. They were described as dedicated, caring, continuous learners, creative, and good communicators among other attributes. Thus, there are studies that not only suggest a consistent image of exemplary teachers, but also that selection of exemplary teachers by peer nomination is a valid method of identification.

Variables of gender, demography, teaching experience, and career intent were also considered. So in addition to participants being considered exemplary by peers, several other criteria were added: female, teaching in an urban setting, at least ten years of classroom experience, and the intent to continue as a classroom teacher. I limited the study to female teachers since the majority of elementary teachers are female. I was curious to know how readily available professional renewal activities would be in a large urban district with inner city problems and a history of failed levies. The ten year experience requirement was an arbitrary boundary to define "veteran" teacher, to allow adequate time for the teacher to have established self-renewal patterns, to have gained considerable experience as a practitioner, and to have become known and identified as exemplary in a school or district. The intention to remain a classroom teacher was included because the study was designed to examine the renewal of exemplary "career teachers," not the minority of teachers who hope to be promoted to an administrative position.

A nomination form (Appendix A) was given to 13 PAR (Peer Assistance and Review) teachers at one of their scheduled meetings. These are teachers who, recognized by their district, have been assigned to work as consulting teachers for beginning teachers or to assist experienced teachers in difficulty. They generally have gained considerable teaching experience in an urban district and, by the nature of their job, get into many schools in their district. In other words, they know a lot of teachers. The nomination forms submitted by the elementary school PAR teachers produced 23 names of potential participants.

From this pool of nominees, I determined the order of solicitation by rank order-
ing the names of teachers by the number of nominations received, highest to lowest.
Starting at the top of the list, I phoned nominees until six participants were found,
six being an arbitrary decision based on time and resources although small samples
are consistent with qualitative research (Miles and Huberman, 1984, p. 36). Even
though the nomination form stipulated the criterion of ten years experience, I discovered at the first interview that one participant had only six years of experience.
Nevertheless, I continued the interview schedule with her since she not only was
already actively involved and recognized professionally at the district level, but also
could serve as an interesting comparison.

Unknown to me at the time of selection and as further evidence of their exemplary nature, the participants have been recognized as exemplary in other ways.
Irene[1] was twice named district Teacher of the Year, while Amy received a Cooperating Teacher Award by a local university. Amy, Camille, and Elizabeth have been
selected as district resource leaders for one or more term appointments. Mary was
honored as her Educational Association's Member of the Year and was also featured
as a television station's Teacher of the Week, selected by the association, administrators, teachers, and students. As well, she was named three times as outstanding
faculty representative in her district and has recently been elected to represent the
district's elementary school teachers as their governor-at-large.

Interviews

Case study researchers commonly "use interviews, qualitative analysis, and narrative reports" (Stake, 1988, p. 256). "[T]he interview is used to gather descriptive
data in the subjects' own words so that the researcher can develop insights on how
subjects interpret some piece of the world" (Bogdan and Biklen, 1992, p. 96). The
purpose of the interview is to capture another person's perceptions or perspectives
and to understand the meaning they attach to their experiences. The interview is a
conversation, "primarily a gift of time and information; and it is given by the re-
spondent, not the interviewer" (Denzin, 1989, p. 109).

Patton (1990) identifies four types of interviews: the informal conversational
interview; the interview guide approach; the standardized open-ended interview;
and the closed, fixed response interview (p. 288-289). These are similar to the
nonstandardized unstructured interview; the nonschedule standardized interview;
and the schedule standardized interview described by Denzin (1989, pp. 104-109).
I selected the interview guide approach (or nonschedule standardized interview) in
which topics and issues to be discussed are outlined in advance. The outline acts as
a checklist but permits complete flexibility of the order and wording of the questions during the interview as well as the opportunity to probe further or ask for
clarification of a response. And while allowing the data collection to be fairly sys-

tematic across responses to facilitate comparison, the interview guide approach nevertheless allows the tone of the interview to remain conversational and situational within a limited time frame (Patton, 1990, pp. 280-288)

In-depth guided interviews were the primary method of data collection; both their strengths and weaknesses were considered. Interviews permit the researcher to collect a lot of data quickly and to seek clarification or amplification on the spot or later. There is the danger, though, that rigid adherence to the scheduled interview topics may result in important themes being inadvertently omitted (Patton, 1990, p. 288). Unless trust and collaboration have been cultivated, participants may withhold data and unless methods of checking accuracy have been incorporated into the research design, the data may be distorted (Marshall and Rossman, 1989, pp. 82-83). And, as Denzin (1989) explained, there is always the possibility in qualitative research that "the knowledge that one is being observed, or interviewed, leads to a deliberate monitoring of the self so that only certain selves are presented" (p. 116-117).

The participants were given the guided interview schedules (Appendix B) for the three 2 1/2 hour interviews ahead of time. Prior to the second interview, they also received a list of possible professional development activities for teachers (Appendix C) which was compiled from the literature and the results of a focus group interview during the pilot study mentioned earlier. The list was offered as a method of stimulating recall and reflection of the participants' professional renewal throughout their career, not as definitive or limiting possibilities for development. The participants were encouraged to expand the list and they added activities such as being a member of the district negotiating team, leader of a teaching team or division, being left "in charge" of the school when the principal was absent, being responsible for organizing a conference, and being involved in union roles.

Each interview was tape recorded and transcribed verbatim before the next interview was conducted. This allowed for clarification or elaboration of comments and for adding questions not on the guided interview schedules.

Instruments

The OCDQ-RE Questionnaire is an Organizational Climate Description Questionnaire for Elementary Schools (see Hoy, Tarter, and Kottkamp, 1991, pp. 160-161). It was designed to examine teachers' perceptions of their school climate. Three specific dimensions of the principal's behavior (supportive, directive, restrictive) and three dimensions of the teachers' behavior (collegial, intimate, disengaged) are identified. (These are elaborated further in chapter 4.) Two other dimensions of school climate are defined. The first dimension, openness in principal behavior, is operationally defined as concern for teachers and their ideas, encouragement of teachers to experiment and be independent, and the reduction of impediments that can interfere with teaching. The second dimension, openness in teacher behavior, is defined to include meaningful and tolerant interactions, support for a cohesive network of social relationships, and acceptance of and respect for colleagues' professional competence (pp. 155-171). These are indicators of organizational health. The developers of the questionnaire proffer the instrument as having heuristic potential, but recognize the limitations in trying to "untangle this seamless web of intervening variables" of organizational climate (p. 153).

Data Analysis

"Data analysis is the process of systematically searching and arranging [data] . . . to increase your own understanding of them and to enable you to present what you have discovered to others" (Bogdan and Biklen, 1992, p. 153). Decisions of which data "to code, which to pull out, which patterns summarize a number of chunks, what the evolving story is, *are all analytic choices*" (Miles and Huberman, 1984, p. 21). However, qualitative research methodology has been criticized for not having "agreed-on canons for qualitative data analysis, in the sense of shared ground rules for drawing conclusions and verifying their sturdiness" (p. 16). Although methodologists generally agree that data analysis is a process of organizing and synthesizing descriptive data into supported conclusions, they do not agree on terminology, as Lincoln and Guba (1985) point out:

> The process of data analysis, then, is essentially a synthetic one, in which the constructions that have emerged (been shaped by) inquirer-source interactions are reconstructed into meaningful wholes. Data analysis is thus not a matter of data *reduction*, as is frequently claimed, but of *induction*. (p. 333)

The following procedure was followed for the data analysis of this study: coding, summary data displays, and identification of themes (Miles and Huberman, 1984).

Procedure

In a sense, the broad categories forming the guided interview schedules could be considered the first level of coding or, as Goetz and LeCompte (1984) describe it, "typologies [which] may be devised from a theoretical framework or set of propositions or from commonsense or mundane perceptions of reality" (p. 183). Initial analysis involved adding new categories. For example, after the first set of interviews, the importance of a sense of professionalism emerged and was added to the second interview schedule.

Closer scrutiny and further coding of the data added new categories, but merged others. For example, I originally split the category of "collegial network" into "collegiality" and "network" since the participants differentiated between colleagues with whom they teach and colleagues who specifically help them in more political ways. I merged "enabling factors" and "constraining factors" into "factors affecting renewal" as the teachers illustrated how the same factors can be both enabling and constraining depending on the context.

During the analysis, summary data displays were also organized. From this second level of coding, themes emerged as the data were recoded within categories. The first display, a chart, resulted in recognition of patterns requiring new codes, such as "school transfers." Another form of data display organized all of the data coded with a particular heading into a single computer file. Data were then searched again with particular attention to anomalies, to alternative explanations, or to competing conclusions. Quotations were selected to capture the context and support conclusions so that readers might judge the transferability of the meaning and interpretation of the data.

Trustworthiness

Quantitative research has long had strict standards of reliability and validity by which to judge the rigor and credibility of studies, but validity criteria in qualitative research are still being debated by such theorists as Lincoln and Guba (1989) and Kvale (1989). Lincoln and Guba (1985) have for some years been applying criteria that are similar to those of the traditional paradigm or "hard" sciences to qualitative research, although they are now rethinking the issues of trustworthiness or authenticity for qualitative research.

Their former criteria are called "parallel" criteria since "they are intended to parallel the rigor criteria that have been used within the conventional paradigm for many years" (Lincoln and Guba, 1989, p. 233). The parallel criteria include:

1. transferability;
2. confirmability (through the arguments put forth and by means of an audit trail);
3. credibility (prolonged engagement, persistent observation, peer debriefing, negative case analysis, progressive subjectivity, member checks, and triangulation depending on the research method employed). (pp. 237-243)

Transferability and the researcher's arguments call for readers' judgment. Care has been taken to keep an audit trail should it be requested. The credibility criteria were dealt with in the following manner to attempt to overcome, at least in part, the danger of subjective bias in qualitative research.

Triangulation

First, I employed methods triangulation (Patton, 1990) which checks out "the consistency of findings generated by different data collection methods" (p. 464). The school climate questionnaire was given to see whether the questionnaire results supported the narrative references in the interview transcripts and to provide a different perspective on the relationship of school climate and renewal. Since I was trying to elicit the teachers' perceptions of their school climate and its influence on their decisions to remain in or leave various environments, it was not necessary to find out whether the participants' perceptions accurately reflected the perceptions of the school staff as a whole.

Although a "reality check" might have been interesting, I wanted to honor my agreement to guarantee anonymity of the participants so they could speak freely about their principals and school climate without fear of reprisal and without compromising what might be important factors constraining their renewal. Both complementary and contradictory results contributed to the patterns in the analysis. For example, as elaborated in chapter 4, the teachers transferred out of a school if the prevailing beliefs of colleagues there clashed with their own. In that case, the principal became a factor in the decision to stay or leave. In cohesive school climates, the principal was not a factor in the teachers' decision to stay in the school.

There was an unanticipated triangulation method as I discovered that five of my participants had worked together. Three had taught at Maplewood School at the same time near the beginning of their careers; three taught at Manchester School; two currently teach together at Black Creek School. One participant was the mentor of the youngest participant in her first year of teaching; they still remain friends. Four know each other through summer curriculum writing teams for the district; two became friends over several summers of writing. Because each participant openly named schools and colleagues during the interviews (unaware that some colleagues they named were also participants), I was able to compare their stories of perceptions of the school and their renewal experiences and check for consistency.

I also employed "analyst triangulation" (Patton, 1990, p. 464) or "peer debriefing" (Lincoln and Guba, 1985, pp. 308-309). This involves multiple analysts to review data and/or interpretations. Four colleagues, who are part-time graduate students and full-time teachers, took the role of peer debriefers. One is a second year teacher while the others each have twenty or more years of experience. One peer debriefer read a set of three interviews for a single participant. The second peer debriefer read all the transcripts for the first interview schedule; the third read all the second interview transcripts; and the fourth read all responses to the final interview.

The four peer debriefers then met with me individually to discuss various interpretations of the data and areas that were puzzling to me.

Each of the peer debriefers, prior to their individual two or three hour meeting with me, had prepared extensive notes which we discussed from their perspective. They were able to provide four different perspectives based on their backgrounds. For example, the second year teacher gave me feedback on the feasibility of the participants' vision of professional development for beginning teachers. The first peer debriefer, trained in psychology and counselling, was able to clarify the importance of specific formative experiences the participants had shared. I also asked the peer debriefers for comments on patterns and interpretations I was considering. For example, I discovered that each had independently come to the conclusion that Irene appeared to be an outlier. I had thought that my conclusion in that regard might reflect researcher bias.

Finally, as part of the credibility criterion, I conducted three member checks with the participants following data analysis. Miles and Huberman (1984) call participants the "most logical source of corroboration" but warn that, because they are a single informant, they may not agree with the researcher's conclusions (p. 242). There were no major disagreements. The first member check dealt only with a skeleton interpretation of the professional renewal section. For the second check, the participants read chapter 4 and gave me written and/or oral feedback. The final check was a discussion of the analysis and implications with each participant.

Validity

Moving beyond the parallel criteria, Lincoln and Guba's (1989) more recent emphasis is on determining a standard of rigor appropriate to the interpretive paradigm, but freed from copying the standards of rigor of the positivist paradigm and freed from being "primarily methodological criteria. That is, they [parallel criteria] speak to methods that can ensure one has carried out the process correctly . . . . Outcome, product, and negotiation are equally important in judging a given inquiry" (p. 245). This is not to say that the more familiar parallel criteria are not important. They are, but having different criteria for the two paradigms is reasonable given that they differ on the fundamental issues of epistemology, ontology, and methodology.

What would validity criteria look like if they were meaningful and designed for appropriateness for qualitative research in education? Kvale's (1989) examination of the issue of validity may be summarized in his following questions:

1. Does the method reflect the phenomenon and investigate what it intends to investigate?
2. Do the results reflect the complexity of the participants' social world?

3. Do the results contribute to new understanding and are they valuable to the group under study (e.g., elementary teachers)?
4. Is the interpretation sound and defensible? (pp. 73-92)

These were the questions I kept in mind as I approached the task of presentation of data, interpretation, and possible implications.

A Caveat Concerning Exemplary Teachers

It is easier to be professional teachers than to share our lives as persons.
To permit our life to be a resource for another's learning is to be
vulnerable to compassion.

(Westerhoff, 1987, p. 193)

As I got feedback from my peer debriefers, themselves teachers and learners, I began to wonder whether expectations of exemplary teachers are too high or unrealistic. The peer debriefers questioned perceived inconsistencies in the beliefs of one participant and wondered how two participants, one perceived as too controlling, the other as insecure, could be called exemplary.

Their initial reactions raise some interesting points. First, being an exemplary teacher does not mean that one has reached a magic pinnacle and that there is little or no room for further improvement and growth. Nor does it mean that these human beings are exempt from inconsistencies, idiosyncrasies, errors of judgment, imperfections, or the limitations of background experiences. As Berliner (1986) cautioned, the performance of expert and experienced teachers, "though not necessarily perfect," can still provide us with "exemplary performances from which we can learn" (p. 6). Another explanation may be related to teachers' high expectations of peers: One of the participants, in discussing her nervousness before conducting a workshop for her colleagues, described peer judgment as "very, very hard."

Second, the issue of remembering a teacher as *not* exemplary does not exclude the possibility of that teacher *becoming* exemplary or being exemplary in some areas. For example, one of the participants, Irene, was assigned this year to teach with Amy, a colleague she had not worked with since they were both beginning teachers. Irene remembered Amy as a novice teacher having problems in her personal and professional life and did not give her credit for growing and changing during the intervening 15 years. Amy openly described her difficult early years as a teacher:

All those beginning years of my teaching — I feel that I always had an essence of communicating with the kids, getting ideas across — but being a good teacher? — absolutely not yet. Not at that point. I think I had rapport. I think they [students] learned, but I was *not* a good teacher as of that time. I had good traits, good things to build on and I don't think the kids suffered too horribly because I did a lot of good things. But as far as calling myself a really good teacher, absolutely not yet.

So while her peer has an outdated image or opinion, Amy's current colleagues see her very differently because she has changed and grown over the intervening years. Even so, she believes there is still a great deal left for her to learn.

I started to see what learning was, that it was a continual process.... I want them [students] to know that there's never a point in your life when you're going to have all the answers. And I'm *not* that person, but I'm a person that can guide children to find a lot of them. ... I have to give an inservice [on teaching writing] to these brand new teachers, and I'm going to tell them this. I'm going to say, "I've been doing this for twenty years. For a period of time, teaching writing was my only job, and it took until two weeks ago for me to feel as successful with it as I ever have. And I don't think I'm probably at the end of where I'm going with it *yet*! The children wrote better than I've ever had a group start a story, and this is [only] the beginning of the year!" So these kids are headed great places with this. But something different happens within *me* too.

The opposite case, that of being considered an exemplary teacher and then temporarily struggling with teaching because of a grade or school transfer or perhaps personal tragedy is another possibility. However, the six participants, in a particular school or grade level and judged on the merits of their most recent years of teaching, were nominated by their colleagues as exemplary. Additionally, five of the participants have received district awards and/or have served in various resource leadership roles at the district level. Three have also been honored as Outstanding Teacher, Outstanding Cooperating Teacher, or district Teacher of the Year. Such recognition does not mean that what these teachers believe or do is *always* exemplary. They are keenly aware of their own performance:

There are days that I wish I never had. It's not all wonderful and there are days when I'm probably the worst teacher out there in the school system. But I'm willing to admit that, and I try and learn from it and improve as much as I can.

These teachers have opened their lives to scrutiny, aware of their limitations and frailties, knowing that they do not live up to their own (and perhaps their colleagues') ideals, but they are willing to continue to strive for improvement.

Summary

Chapter 3 provided a rationale for using a qualitative research design for this study and described the case study method. The method of selection and a description of the interviews and questionnaire followed. Finally, analysis of the data was elaborated, along with a caveat concerning exemplary teachers. Chapter 4 is a presentation of the themes that emerged from the data and a discussion of the findings.

CHAPTER IV
FINDINGS

This chapter begins with brief "impressionistic" sketches of the six participants in this study: Mary, Elizabeth, Irene, Amy, Camille, and Donna. However, the entire chapter should be considered as a portrait in order for the reader to understand the teachers more holistically and to appreciate the complexity of their lives.

These teachers were nominated by their peers as exemplary: Colleagues described them as innovative, creative, flexible, caring, child oriented, nurturing, continuing to develop professionally, dedicated, positive, motivating, and excellent communicators. They have also been recognized in various other ways. Elizabeth, Amy, and Camille have been selected by their district for one or more term appointments as a resource leader. Amy was honored with an award for Outstanding Cooperating Teacher, a tribute from a local university based on nominations by student teachers. Irene, Camille, Amy, and Donna have been invited to present at conferences by university faculty members or district coordinators. Irene was twice named district Teacher of the Year. Mary was nominated by union representatives, administrators, teachers, and students to be featured as an Outstanding Teacher on a television station. She has also been named three times in her career as Outstanding Faculty Representative for the district and once as the UEA's (Urbanville Educational Association) Member of the Year and national delegate. She recently won an election by the district's elementary teachers to represent them as governor-at-large.

The chapter is designed to respond to the research questions stated in chapter 1. The questions are:

1. What are exemplary teachers' beliefs about teaching/learning and are these related to their renewal?
2. How do exemplary teachers self-renew personally and professionally?

3. Is there an expanding scope of professional awareness, involvement, and contribution throughout their career? (e.g., classroom, school, district, state, national, international)
4. Which personal and contextual factors enable and/or constrain their renewal?
5. How do exemplary teachers deal with constraints on their renewal?
6. What are their visions for improving professional development for teachers?

The chapter elaborates formative experiences of the participants, common experiences as beginning teachers, the participants' beliefs about teaching/learning, their personal and professional renewal, factors enabling and/or constraining their renewal, their ethic of care, commitment, and their suggestions for improving teachers' professional development.

"Impressionistic" Sketches of the Teacher Participants

Mary

A parrot squawked excitedly and two enormous dogs erupted through the door simultaneously, eyes alight and tails thudding in joyous welcome. Mary was home from school. Her soothing voice was almost drowned out in the happy din as each pet vied for her attention. I glanced around the room, intrigued by the art and objets d'art everywhere, the unusual plants, the books and magazines, a guitar.

As Mary began to tell her story, I was riveted by her rhythmic, melodious voice, not surprised to find out she is a soloist. Her words are carefully chosen, a habit refined by years of practice as a faculty representative and contract negotiator. Only the slightest lift of an eyebrow or hint of a dimple accompanies a droll sense of humor or dry understatement.

A neighbor tiptoed through the open door, grinning as he set a bag of groceries on the counter. "For the party tomorrow," he whispered gaily. "Very social," Mary's lilting voice was saying as she winked a thank-you to him and absently stroked the mastiff's head resting on her knee. "I've always just been very social."

Elizabeth

My heels sank into the white carpet as I walked into the quiet calm of the living room. A perfectly balanced plate of crackers, cheese, and olives waited on a polished endtable, flanked by a collector plate, books, and music cassettes. Sun filtered through gauze-like curtains on to the grand piano and magnificent grandfather clock dominating the room.

Settling into the sofa, Elizabeth started to talk. Her hands waved animatedly as she punctuated a torrent of words interrupted only by peals of frequent laughter. My pen flew across the page as she whizzed from France to Puerto Rico, from concerts to books, from friends to students, from cooking to theater.

Elizabeth's gift for amusing storytelling was interrupted by the measured bongs of the clock. "More coffee?" she asked, ever the practiced hostess, as she launched into a tale that sent us both into gales of laughter.

Irene

There was a quiet tap on my door. "I'm sorry I'm late," said Irene with an apologetic smile. "I had to take the kids home first." Her voice picked up as she talked warmly about her own children and her school "children." Her big, dark, expressive eyes clouded in reminiscing about her high school years, danced as she grinned in recalling creative antics with a close colleague, shone as she discussed her son's latest computer project.

I struggled to comprehend the powerful ties of a family and community closely knit by religion and ethnicity. Irene's eyes helped me to understand immigrant, work, financial struggle, sacrifice, love, and pride. Her voice dropped to a murmur. "Oh, yes," she breathed. "Education is very important. I was the first to graduate from college, you know."

Amy

Amy's lithe frame, flattered by a thoroughly modern outfit, glided across the room toward the divan. She casually crossed her long legs and leaned back comfortably. Her strong, confident voice jolted my attention to her face: eyes always alight with anticipation and an expectant look that seems to say, "Hi, world! Here I am! Show me what interesting curiosity you have for me today."

"A pixie face," I thought, "yet amazingly, a face with the kind of character that is only sculpted through hardship or tragedy and great personal courage." A desire to learn . . . a need for people, but also for solitude . . . athletic grace . . . inner strength . . . "Turn the tape recorder off," she said with a confirming nod, "and I'll tell you."

Camille

Five of us converged in the living room at the same time. With a calm, no-fuss style, Camille somehow managed to clear the room so we could begin the first interview. Stacks of books balanced everywhere, school work begged for attention, a basketball and a pair of ballet slippers lounged under the piano bench. Camille caught my eye and laughed. "You should see the garage and basement," she smiled with a shrug. "I have boxes and boxes of school things."

The phone rang. It was the parent of a student. Then at last, we were ready to begin. Camille looked like a tiny doll as she tucked her feet under her and, with a smile, focussed unwavering attention on my questions. Her physical composure belied the lightning speed of her quiet voice as I followed her through four states and a lifetime packed with intense energy, enthusiasm, and education.

Donna

Donna's honey-colored hair and crimson corduroy slacks made a splash of color against the pale, immaculate decor of the family room. Sitting cross-legged, elbows resting on a plush cushion in her lap and hands propping up her chin, she laughed at the childish handwriting of her composition announcing, "When I grow up, I want to be a teacher."

As she talked about teaching, Donna's clear, commanding voice flowed across her school work neatly organized for later attention, recent books and magazines stacked tidily on the glass coffee table, and frames of patiently worked cross-stitching displayed attractively around the room. Following her gaze to the Green lawn and flowers bathed in a fading autumn sunset, I heard Donna's voice drop as she admired the view. "This renews me," she reflected. "It takes a lot of energy to work with kids in the inner city. But I give it my best shot for their sake. They've got a lot rougher life than any of us have ever had. I'm willing to give them 110% because they deserve it."

Formative experiences

Teachers' experiences prior to their college courses in teacher education are rarely accounted for in the literature. Only recently have some researchers studied teachers' biographies in an effort to understand teachers and their teaching in a more holistic way (e.g., Goodson, 1992). The participants in this study spoke willingly of their memories of elementary and high school, their family's attitudes toward education, and their own relationships with memorable teachers.

School Days

Two of the participants, Mary and Irene, attended parochial schools, but their experiences were quite different. Mary remembers that she was always a good student, but that math was difficult despite her effort. "I remember working really hard for my eighth grade math teacher. Math was not one of the things that I felt very comfortable in. Being a girl, I was not pushed into that. I always had sort of like a complex about it." Nevertheless, her ability in school was recognized by her teachers. "The nuns would come across to take me out of class to watch their classes while they had to do something. It was like I had 'teacher' [laugh] across my forehead. . . . The teachers that I had were very supportive. One teacher let a group of us out of study hall and we would discuss all sorts of social problems."

It was social interactions that Mary remembers clearly. She was "a chubby, heavy kid" and was very self-conscious, particularly when she changed schools and got a lot of negative comments from her new schoolmates. "It really upset me the first year and I let it upset me and then the next year, I thought, 'Well if they don't like me, too bad!' I went on and I did all right [laugh] and I became everybody's friend." She was also fortunate to have "an unusual principal" when she changed schools. "Of course I didn't know anybody. The principal took an interest in me and he always stopped me and asked me how I was doing and put his arm around me and said, 'You know, if there's anything I can do . . .' and just kept making sure I was okay and fitting in." Surviving the experience, Mary went on to become very involved in a variety of extra-curricular activities, including drama, photography, and Future Teachers of America.

As a teacher, Mary is alert to the social adjustment of students, even before they are assigned to her classroom.

> When children hurt each other by words, it just tears me apart. I had one student who was asked if she was pregnant because she was a really roly-poly kind of a child. This girl was so bright, so intelligent. When I watched her in third grade, I noticed that she would rather read in the room than go out to play. So when she came to me in fourth grade, I scooted her out every single day and her mother thanked me for that because she really didn't deal with the other children. Her world was the books, where she could shut out those kids.

Mary's parents wanted her to go to college. Her perception is that since her siblings had dropped out, she was her parents' last hope. They paid for her first year of college after which Mary, thanks to her high grades, was able to get a renewable student loan.

Irene did not seem to enjoy the same kind of support from her teachers as Mary did.

> I don't really remember loving school [laugh], but I never hated it. I enjoyed learning, but I was often bored — not because of the content, just uninteresting methods of presenting the content probably. I would daydream, fall asleep often. I had problems in high school [with science and math] and was even told perhaps I should not go to college, that I should consider another field — was not encouraged to apply for a scholarship. When I went in to ask the guidance counsellor for information material, he said, "Oh, those

books along the wall" and I was just overwhelmed and left and never applied for anything. I was an "A" student once I entered the College of Education my Junior year. But because my math and science background is *so* poor, for a variety of reasons, if I *had* to take the teacher exam, I don't know that I'd pass.

Irene spoke several times about her enjoyment of creative writing, but the need to have her written work "polished" by members of her family and later, colleagues who were good at spelling and editing. Irene had no role models encouraging her to attend college and understood that as a female within a closely-knit ethnic family, she was expected to live at home until she married. This, and not having a scholarship, limited her choices of universities and colleges. Ignoring her guidance counsellor's advice, she applied to the same local university as her best friend and worked her way through college.

I was never *dis*couraged from going to college, but I was never really encouraged or pushed. My parents were very interested in what I did; they wanted me to do well in school, but they never pushed. My grandparents would never have told me to go to college because they didn't understand giving all that money away. I mean, even though there was no money there, everything else was totally around me and school. Mom would have a hot dinner and she'd do my laundry and my parents would drive me to the library late at night to study.

Even though Irene does not think she had particularly good teachers, she "played teacher" on weekends as an adolescent. She ran a Saturday morning "school" in her garage for pre-school neighborhood children, charging a dime per child to pay for a snack and activity. She also enjoyed babysitting and taking young cousins downtown to attend puppet plays. From a young age, Irene's life seems to have revolved around family, school, and children and the pattern has continued.

Unlike Irene, Donna felt very comfortable with the idea of going to college since her father was a college professor and she had other relatives in education. In addition to maintaining an "A" average through school and college, she was heavily involved in extra-curricular activities.

School wasn't just academics for me; it was also a social place, just a fun place to be. I had a lot of extracurricular activities — like being in the guidance office, or being the manager of a sports team, or being on a sports team. I mean, there were times when I hated school, you know, but on the whole when I look back, I feel very good about the education I got.

Donna also seemed to have comfortable out-of-school relationships with some of her teachers. "I keep in touch with some of my teachers still — even from elementary school. In middle school, I babysat for a lot of the teachers and I went on family vacations with them to do babysitting." She also felt at ease with her parents' friends and colleagues and with making her views known to older siblings. "That's kind of how I was brought up with adults. I was taught to respect them, but I didn't have to be intimidated." Her rapport with teaching colleagues was noticed when she began to practice teach. As a young teacher, she is also not intimidated presenting workshops to older veteran teachers.

Amy's father too became a college professor after years of teaching high school. Amy always knew she would continue a long family tradition of going to college.

> I never considered *not* going to college. I come from a very strong "value education" background for generations on my father's side. I had a great-grandfather that was a teacher, so I was very comfortable with it from my own family background. I had very educated great-grandparents; it was quite rare at the time. And then my father went to school during the Depression and became a teacher. I was an "A" student all the way through. Very academic-oriented, achievement oriented, very competitive. I was no brain child or genius child or anything. Didn't always come easy. I worked very hard and I got good grades right through college too and achieved and have always felt successful.

However, despite high achievement, Amy knew she did not do well on multiple choice tests, a requirement for college entry. "They told me not to bother going to college when I took the ACT (American College Test). I looked at that man and said, "Excuse *me!*" To this day, Amy is passionately opposed to single measures of assessment and multiple choice tests.

Amy remembers three exemplary grade school teachers who influenced her as a person and as a teacher.

> From my third grade teacher, I learned compassion. She's the teacher who rushed over to my house after school — we had been knitting candy canes that day. She'd counted needles at the end of the day and searched her memory bank and was sure I had left a needle on my candy cane and was afraid that I was going to get hurt. She came over seeking this needle, just to see if I was okay. Compassionate. Loving. Her whole countenance was just [pause] nurturing. Then I hit fourth grade and I remember doing these wonderful projects. I just remember being excited about learning that year. I remember the papier- mâché planets that we made — and I have trouble with teach-

ers doing what I call "the grandiose projects" that I'm not sure there's been much learning benefit. But we researched those planets and we worked out how to create them. First, we tried to just do them with balloons and they collapsed. We had this wire and we had to solve how to build these planets. I had Saturn and I had to figure out how to put these rings on Saturn. It was real problem solving and giving reports and all that. There was a lot more learning going on than making papier-mâché planets. Fifth grade, I probably had the most marvelous teacher — again, projects. Good teacher — you didn't mess with Miss Calvin — and good nurturing, but not in the same way as the third grade teacher. The third grade teacher was the hugs and the kisses and the caring and the mother hen. Miss Calvin nurtured and "You will grow up or else" and "You can do this. I know it" — firm belief in you, and that's the bottom line. And I'm probably a lot more like Miss Calvin. I nurture and I hug, but it's more "You can do this" and "We *will* do this and I'm going to show you how and I'm there every step of the way for you."

Today, as in her fourth and fifth grade experiences, Amy likes to teach around themes and problem solving, making sure that children understand the process of learning.

Like Amy, Camille also knew she would go to college. She too got high grades and enjoyed school. In addition to her father wanting her to be a teacher, Camille also had some good role models and special relationships with teachers.

I had an older cousin who was a teacher, a Special Education teacher, and I kind of idolized her and just kind of wanted to be like her when I was a little girl. I guess I had a lot of really good teachers. I think each one offered something different and unique and I guess they pulled things out of me and inspired me to stay in education and to keep up with education. In high school — oh, I had a speech teacher that I liked a lot and a drama teacher that I liked a lot. For some reason, there were always personal relationships — more than just a teacher-student relationship. And it wasn't only with just me; it was with a lot of the kids — that you got to know the teachers on a more personal level as well. They spent a lot of time with us. In high school, I was the business manager of the yearbook and so I was working with the teacher in charge of that and it's a different kind of relationship.

As early as high school, Camille's love of literature, the theater, and the arts was evident. As a teacher, she weaves them into her curriculum and tries to share her love of literature and the arts with her students, frequently taking her young students on field trips to concerts and performances. She also relies on reading and the arts for personal relaxation.

Elizabeth's parents, though separated, both taught her to value education. She recalls getting mostly "B" and some "A" grades in elementary and high school. There was never any doubt she would go to college: "I mean, no matter what! My parents were going to find a way for us to go to college. They were always supportive about school. They paid the part that the scholarship didn't take care of so I never *had* to work unless I wanted to." Elizabeth's grades slipped drastically when, in her first year of college, she chose a number of science courses because she was thinking about being a nurse.

> I only had a 2.8 GPA (Grade Point Average)[2] at the end of my first year. I started doing the chemistry and the biology and I didn't like the courses and I didn't want to study for the courses. And I was having too much fun! I had a 3.8 [GPA] when I graduated 'cause once I got into the professional school and I was taking education courses, I was taking courses I really worked for.

Today, more than twenty years later, Elizabeth is still taking math and science inservice courses to improve her teaching ability in these two areas which she considers to be her weakest teaching subjects.

Like Mary, Elizabeth too was a member of Future Teachers of America in high school. On occasion, when a substitute teacher could not be found for the Latin class, Elizabeth was recommended by the regular teacher to "take over the class." Two high school teachers encouraged her to enter teaching, even though she was quite determined to go into nursing. In retrospect, she believes her decision not to be a teacher was an attempt to be different from her sister who had always had teaching in mind. Elizabeth recalls having had some other teachers who were influential role models, both in and out of the classroom.

> Mrs. DiLucio was a real good influence on me and I liked — I mean, she was always very personal; she tried to find out something about each student and tried to talk to them about that area of interest. She was the "Y" teen advisor and I was the president and I worked with her. She ran the movies in the gym and so she'd always let me help her on that and I got to pick the movies and stuff like that. So I think a lot of that was that personal touch of trying to find something nice about each child and trying to help them bring that out 'cause she always would try to encourage me. When I was in elementary school, I remember Mrs. O'Neill. She was not a humorous woman, but she always had a smile for you. Very positive type person — and the way she would talk to you! I wish I were more like her! She would just turn

64

[conflicts] around on us and make us think and try to encourage problem solving — "Now, let's think about that action. Did that help?" You know, very calm. So I try to remember her when she was doing things like that and that's what I try to do when there's a fight between kids.

A Work Ethic

In one form or another, each of the participants share the same work ethic, that of doing their best. Irene learned that "if you truly believe in something, if it's *that* important, it has to be done right." Elizabeth explained what was meant by "doing it right" or "doing your best."

> My Dad always said, "If you intend to get ahead anywhere, you *must* do a good job." I feel that if there's something new out there and I can do something better, then I should learn how to do something better rather than just sitting and stewing about it. That's why I tend to want to go for an inservice or training, see someone, speak to someone, anything that will help me make it better.

This drive to do one's best is always present. Donna would like to resign as committee chair because she does not feel it's right for her to continue unless she can give the time and do the job the way she thinks it should be done. Camille commented that although she may have begun by doing her best for her parents, by the time she got to high school, doing a top quality job was to please herself. Now as a teacher, she says, "Even though there are long hours and there's lots of take-home work, I like it. I couldn't do something I didn't like and I couldn't devote the amount of time that I devote to this were I not happy. You know, I guess you kind of thrive on it." Doing their best in teaching gives meaning to these teachers' lives.

Discussion

As Lortie (1975) pointed out, children have years and years over which to observe teachers. Five of the participants remembered some wonderful teachers and three specifically linked what they do in their own classrooms with what they learned from those teachers. Additionally, through babysitting for teachers or working with them in extracurricular activities, they learned to see and know those teachers differently — as a person with a life and personality outside the classroom.

The participants' experiences as students prior to becoming teachers appear to have influenced them considerably: They absorbed values, decided to emulate certain teachers' styles or dispositions, and set personal patterns of involvement and learning. From their parents, they learned a work ethic that not only impels them to do their best, but also involves learning "how to do something better" and the habit of capitalizing on "anything that will help [them] make it better." The connections drawn by the participants between their present and past suggests that examining biographies of preservice teachers may provide important clues about the formation of dispositions and decisions to become a teacher. Biographies may also clarify possible links between teachers' work ethic, learning, and commitment.

Becoming a Teacher

Distinctive Preservice Experiences

As part of the Future Teachers of America program offered in high schools, both Mary and Elizabeth had opportunities to go into elementary schools to work with children and to do little teaching projects. The other participants all had preservice teaching experiences that were considered unusual at the time, either because they were being offered as special or experimental programs, or because the time of teaching (e.g., in Junior instead of Senior year) and length of time spent in the schools was uncommon compared to the regular preservice programs being offered.

Donna did her practice teaching in her Junior year in a new program that emphasized literature-based learning. Her practice teaching was in an alternative school considered to be "informal." Amy participated in a special urban education project during her Senior year. It was the sixties and the civil rights movement was headline news.

A lot of speakers came in. I did my student teaching in a very inner city area of [a major city], and we were in the schools more than we would have been if we'd gone through the regular [teacher preparation] program at the time. So I had more firsthand experience and was really talked to about the inner city experience and what to prepare for.

Camille was assigned to an inner city school in a metropolis during each semester of her final year in college. For the first semester, she spent a half day on campus and the other half day in the school, either observing or later, teaching on a limited basis. The last half of the year was spent student teaching in the same school. Only Amy and Camille had inner city training built into their preservice program. However, all of the teachers except Mary later taught in inner city schools.

Irene, like Donna, was in a special program that allowed her to do her practice teaching in her Junior year and she too was trained in an informal school. Additionally, the program required attendance on campus for only one day per week, permitting students to spend four days in a school each week throughout the school year, including ten weeks of student teaching in the same school. She felt very comfortable at her assigned school.

It was not an alternative school when I went there but it had a group of parents who were very interested in making it an alternative school. They were on the forefront, because they really believed in the philosophy of informal education and they wanted to have their children have the opportunity of staying with teachers who had that type of philosophy: a non-traditional, informal, open classroom.

She liked the school well enough that during her Senior year, when she was not on campus, she volunteered to run an enrichment program at the school. There was no course of study, so she created interesting activities for the small groups of students she worked with. When a maternity leave had to be filled from March to June at the school, the position was offered to Irene. And because the outgoing teacher was to have taken a student teacher from March to June, the student teacher was assigned to Irene who had graduated as a certified teacher just one week earlier.

Common Experiences as Beginning Teachers
Five participants shared the following experiences within the first seven years of their career:

1. teaching in an open space area;
2. team teaching;
3. having opportunities to observe other teachers;
4. conducting parent/teacher conferences jointly with one or more teachers;
5. teaching a multi-age group or the same group of children for two or more consecutive years;
6. voluntarily and/or involuntarily changing grades, assignments, and schools quite frequently.

The sixth participant, Donna, had similar experiences. She shared her classroom with a half time partner teacher for the first three years of her career as she concentrated on being a language arts teacher (half time in a first grade classroom and half time working as a reading recovery teacher with individual or small groups of children). Wanting to get experience in seeing children develop more holistically, she and another teacher asked to teach all subjects to a multi-age group they could work with for two or more years. When their request to remove the wall between their classrooms was denied, they continued team planning instead of team teaching. Because Donna was trained as a reading recovery teacher early in her career, she had opportunities to observe many other teachers and to be observed by them. She also had had people observing her regularly during her student teaching days because she was in an informal school.

Teaching at Maplewood School

Amy, Irene, and Elizabeth taught at Maplewood School very early in their careers. Maplewood was an experimental school in the seventies and was known for its open space and multi-age grouping of students. Teachers were given special training, particularly in team teaching, team evaluation techniques, meeting effectiveness, and curriculum writing. They were encouraged to experiment and innovate.

Because of the open space, the teachers had constant opportunities to observe each other, share materials and ideas, and talk together. Since the school was considered unusual for the district, there was a steady flow of visitors and parents in the building. The teachers became accustomed to "being on stage" and speaking to large groups of adults, especially to explain their curriculum to parents.

While the participants mentioned the problems that can and did occur in an open space school, the value of their experiences there cannot be underestimated.

Maplewood was a *very* good learning experience. I know I already had my Master's [degree], but I don't care: I didn't learn nearly as much from it as from Maplewood. I feel that it was a really important time for me as a teacher because it stretched me a lot to work on a team like that, to learn to design curriculum and learning centers, to learn to work with a multi-age group of children, and to learn to work in a space where you had no space. Everything was shared and we had so many teachers from such a variety of backgrounds. Plus we got to go visit other schools like ours. (Elizabeth)

I worked at Maplewood, and it was great. I loved it. It was a magnificent school. I was *thoroughly* trained there. (Amy)

I *loved* it there. It was wonderful because we could really individualize which I could learn from my colleagues and it was wonderful because we really learned each others' strengths. (Irene)

As Irene noted, "Lots of the people who have left Maplewood have gone on in the Urbanville schools to be leaders."

Open space, team teaching, and observation

Of the six common experiences, the participants spoke at greatest length about the impact of teaching in an open space, team teaching, and observation. When they discussed their experiences, they focussed on the positive learning that took place, although difficulties associated with the experience were not dismissed. For example, Irene described her years in an open space area as "the best of times and the worst of times because when somebody had a bad day or somebody was off for maternity leave, we all knew it and we all suffered." Amy said, "Teaming like that, especially when you can watch your team mates all day long is like being married four times over. And we had similar type problems too at times — personality conflicts, different ideas, rest levels. I mean, there were times when we each threatened to take our desks and move and build our little walls."

However, the teachers all look back on their experience in an open space area as one that helped them grow in many ways. Their stories emphasize that their learning was linked to their personal and professional relationships with other teachers.

> I enjoyed the interaction with another teacher. I enjoyed the fact that if I had to leave the room, there was someone who could hear automatically what was going on. I liked the space because you could move in or out of your space: You could move into the library learning center, have some groups out there, and you could hear what was going on even if you were in your room. It was an exciting, exciting time. I think the kids learned an *awful* lot. (Mary)

> I've had a lot of contact with other teachers and observing styles [of teaching]. So whether you realize it or not, subconsciously I was drawing a lot of conclusions, deciding what I wanted to do and what I didn't want to do. (Irene)

> You had to be very considerate of your fellow teachers and we had to plan when our noisy activities were. You also helped your fellow teachers, so when you knew that they were having a bad day by hearing what was going on, then you would send a little note, you know, "It's only an hour before lunch" or "You can make it." Those kind of things, which brought a little levity to the situation and brought you back down to earth . . . and helps you get to know each other as people. I think that what happens a lot of times is we close our door and we go inside and sometimes we tend not to look at what's happening in their lives, you know. They may need an extra hug or an extra pat on the back. (Mary)

> I feel that [working in an open space] was a really important time for me as a teacher because it stretched me a lot. I had to *work* in terms of teaming. I mean, I'd always had *my* class and always done *my* thing. I mean, I had

always been friends with other teachers and we'd gone on trips, we'd switch kids, we'd come up with ideas. But this was living with three people all the time and planning the units together, planning what was going to happen, designing our own curriculum. Everything was shared. It was such a good learning experience because we had so many teachers from such a variety of backgrounds. We just would try things and because you had another person with you, you felt more willing to try it. (Elizabeth)

I think I learned a tremendous amount from that experience. First of all, I know that you can't just say to somebody, "You're going to team teach." You need to really get along with that person and you have to have the same philosophy. And it has to be a give-and-take relationship. A sense of humor is incredibly important. You *have* to be able to laugh. Bernice was my team partner, very warm and open. She shared ideas, she shared suggestions for classroom management and the kind of thing that you're not well prepared for in college. She and I had many conversations and discussions. She was a great help to me and even today, we're still friends. We're still in touch, even though we live far away and don't see each other often. (Camille)

Two specific areas of growth, although they are related, were mentioned frequently: Observing colleagues and being observed by colleagues are both ways of improving one's teaching. Team teaching not only gave these teachers an opportunity to observe peers regularly, but also made them comfortable with being observed by others. The teachers recognized that teaching with other adults taught them to examine and monitor every word and action directed at students. They came to value having adults (teachers or parent volunteers) as a "personal behavior barometer," as a source of humor, as peer evaluators, and as a resource for learning.

But for the most part, I enjoyed — I think [working in an open space] definitely got me over the fear of being watched. I mean, I don't think about it at all when someone walks in my room anymore. If you were going to remain in open space, you just didn't mind being watched. That's all there was to it. And that's why a lot of teachers couldn't take it. I think a lot of people said the noise bothered them, which is partially true. But I think most of it was [that] they couldn't stand the spotlight quite to that degree. You function differently when there's an adult listening to every word you say. (Amy)

It does bring you back to reality when someone's watching you. [When nobody's there], you just say anything. You get mad, you can fly off the handle, you can be mean to a child, demean a child, or you can have the worst lesson in the world 'cause you're just not thinking. You don't have a focus. But have somebody else in that room and you're like, "What would be the best way to get this across?" If you never have the opportunity to see anyone else teach or to have anyone give you feedback on what's going on, then you *don't* tend to improve yourself. You just have no way to improve 'cause you don't know what you're trying to get to be. You don't know what's better. (Elizabeth)

You are forced to see yourself through someone else's eyes — adult teacher eyes. That is definitely critical. I think that you need to stop and think, "Is this really what I want to say?" And it doesn't mean that you're perfect just because you had that experience. But it certainly — I think it's a valuable experience for teachers to have adults listening. That's why it's good to have parents in the room. And it's also good for humor. When something funny happens, sometimes the kids don't get it and you need another adult to appreciate it. (Camille)

The team met and we planned and we self-evaluated. And we had techniques to do that with. At first, we would evaluate ourself as a team; and then each team member would go around [the circle] and we would discuss each other's strengths and weaknesses and get right down to the nitty gritty — talk about functioning as a team and what that takes. We got pretty frank. We really did. It was an open environment. (Amy)

We built into our concept of teaching [the idea of] sharing and being open with other teachers, whereas those teachers who have been closing doors are just totally threatened by anybody or anything that walks through them. So we just had that beat out of us, literally. [laugh] Our whole environment was open. Because as adult teachers, we are going to learn from other adult teachers, you know — you can't close your mind down to that and say, "I'm just going to stay in here with my children." You're playing nursemaid then, and that's not what we're all about. We have to be able to relate with *our* peers in order to keep growing. (Amy)

It is significant that even when these teachers moved to schools with closed classrooms, they ignored the physical walls and found ways of continuing what they had learned to value: team planning, sharing new ideas, and the presence of other adults. Camille found a team partner who was willing to plan activities that allowed Kindergarten and first grade children to work together. Now at another school, she voluntarily team plans with one or more teachers: "The more you get to know someone — you know, if you're doing the same thing, you kind of work with them. So at this point, all of us have been there for a number of years now, and so we do a lot of planning together."

Irene was so lonely in a closed classroom that she too sought out teacher partners or aides as well as parent volunteers to fill the void. She also came up with creative ways to work with teachers, such as volunteering to help them with learning centers in their classrooms and putting on musical productions that involved a lot of staff participation.

> I had my four walls again. After teaching in open space, what I missed was my *friends*. That's probably why I did the [learning] centers, just to go into other people's rooms. I couldn't stand being confined in the classroom. I was very lonely. When I was at the next school, I did team a little with the other Kindergarten teacher. We were a long way apart, but there was one empty classroom for awhile and we would get together and do things in there and we would do the musicals together too. And with my aides, I would kind of use them to bounce things off of, kind of team teaching even if they're not teaching. I'd just say something funny and we'd start laughing and then the kids would crack up. It's nice having somebody else in there and I'm missing that [in a new school this year] because my aide's here [only] an hour and I don't have any parents that I know yet.

Elizabeth recently saw a school plan that would provide time for teachers to observe and give feedback to each other within the school. She would like to see it in her school as well.

> I don't know how it will fly and somebody may file a grievance. Anyway, I thought maybe it would help people to feel closer if they actually did get in and observe and not feel so bad about "I'm in this alone." And I know what happens when I've observed before: You tend not to be mean to a person. You tend to say, "Well, that was nice" and not tell them [more criticism] until you get to know them. On our teams [in the open space school], we could say, "Yuck, maybe if you moved your group over this way, it wouldn't interfere." Or, "When you did this, it messed up my group totally. They lost all control." If we could just get a start on that . . .

She suggests that genuine, frank feedback depends on how well colleagues know each other and that specific techniques to facilitate the feedback process can be learned. Having once learned how to give and take honest criticism and to enjoy teaming, she has continued in subsequent schools to seek out and enjoy people who will undertake projects with her or be her partner.

As a spin-off to team teaching, all of the teachers have had experience with joint parent/teacher conferences and with having the same children for more than one year. Through voluntary or involuntary assignments, they have also experienced different age levels and have had opportunities to understand the curriculum scope and sequence over several grade levels. While they perceive these experiences to have been very valuable and helpful, most of their descriptions of their early experiences focussed on their learning through open space teaching, team teaching, and observation.

Discussion

It is evident that open space and team teaching experiences have had a profound and lasting effect on these teachers. In such an environment, prolonged time together, observation, and evaluation feedback were built-in components that led to joint parent/teacher conferences, teaching the same children for consecutive years, and flexibility "to go with the flow" or innovate. Teachers at Maplewood School were given specific training in human relations, meeting effectiveness, and evaluation/feedback techniques. Visitation to open space schools in other districts was also arranged.

Teaching in front of peers and then giving/receiving constructive criticism was a "shared ordeal" (Howey and Zimpher, 1989) that brought these teachers together by making them be risk takers and vulnerable in front of colleagues. In essence, this was a form of peer coaching. However, there was also team support and, I suspect, mutual respect growing out of learning to know their colleagues well both professionally and personally. They could not avoid different styles of teaching and perspectives and they had to learn to be tactful and thoughtful toward peers.

The teachers recognized that their teaching/learning and their students' learning benefitted from collaboration and that collegial support and ideas were available for the asking. The collegial interaction and support, coupled with the learning that resulted from collaboration, set habits that continued after the teachers left the open space environment. The participants persisted in seeking out colleagues with whom and from whom they enjoyed teaching and learning, regardless of the physical structure of the school. Many lasting friendships developed between team members.

Rosenholtz (1989) noted that teacher learning and collaboration are linked to teacher certainty. (I prefer the term "confidence," given the uncertainty always facing teachers.) This study suggests that peer observation with genuine, honest feedback among teachers builds confidence, encourages trust and respect, and acts as a tool to improve teaching and learning. It surely is not accidental that much of what the veteran teachers envision in an ideal model of professional development is a mirror image of their own early, valued experiences.

Beliefs about Teaching/Learning

I'm thinking of habits of mind — the ways of thinking about children and all the alternative programs have a philosophy that goes with the theme of a combined set of attitudes and beliefs about learners and about yourself as a teacher and the interaction between them.

Barnes (1989, pp. 216-217)

Research question: What are exemplary teachers' beliefs about teaching/learning and are these related to their renewal?

Central to these teachers' practice is a clearly defined set of beliefs about teaching and learning. The participants were able to articulate those core beliefs, beliefs that were remarkably consistent from teacher to teacher. What follows is an experimental text in order to give the teachers "pride of place" so that they might communicate their beliefs to the reader in their own words. Even though the six participants never met together, I have created a contrived conversation among them by piecing together fragments of each person's interviews. The excerpts employed are actual statements, but were not made in a group conversation. I believe this "conversation" is helpful in demonstrating the depth of inquiry, reflection, risk taking, and innovation that the participants willingly and continuously engage in so that they and their students can be both learners and teachers.

On Teaching and Learning

Donna: I believe every child can learn. I have been faced with many [inner city] students who, at first glance, even I doubted that they can progress; but they do. It takes a lot of devotion to it. It takes a lot of tries. It's trial and error. There's going to be things that work and things that don't, and it varies from child to child and class to class.

Mary: Because there are so many different ways to teach and all of them have their points. Not all of them work for any one group of children and you may have to switch gears several times. It is real hard to know what works for every child and sometimes you can't find the thing that works. Or you can't find it fast enough and by then, you're off on the wrong footing with the child and it's too hard to come back.

Donna: You need to know your students, each one of them, and it takes a lot of time and a lot of effort.

Mary: And there are so many children, too, that you see later and you wonder, "Did I do enough?" You always have that: Did I do enough for that kid? You know, was there anything else I could have done that maybe would have turned the key? And I really — I've always been a believer that miracles can happen and you can take some of these kids and really work with them. Sometimes you're dealing with odds totally against your favor. And that again is knowing what you can do and you've got to keep going even though you know. . .

Irene: That's what I tell my student teachers. You can't change the child's home environment so you have to work with them the best way you can. Probably what you do is more than anyone has done before or may do again. Learn to work with the parents. Be accepting, but know you're not going to change the world overnight. Do the best you can for the five hours a day you see that child.

Camille: Exactly. You can't just write off kids because they need to learn. If whatever you're doing doesn't seem to work, you've got to try something else. Hopefully, ultimately, something will click. I believe that it's our job as teachers to find the point at which each child is when they walk into your room, and stretch them as far as you can, up and across. As far as learning goes, while all children can learn, you have to take into consideration developmental stages and find things that are appropriate for those students to learn. I think you have to have goals in mind and not just rumble from thing to thing. I think you need to keep learning styles in mind — that all children don't learn in the same way and the class is composed of all different individuals. So whatever it is you're presenting, you need to present it in more than one way. They need to have hands-on things. You need to give them a chance to interact with you and with one another.

Irene: And some children learn best in individual [instruction] and some learn best through small group instruction and some learn best through large group instruction. So I feel that throughout the day, I should be meeting with children individually, in small groups, and whole groups dependent upon what I'm doing.

Elizabeth: The last few years, I've gotten involved with whole language. I really and truly do believe that that is the way that children will learn and that is the way to teach — in terms of you start from the whole and move toward the parts — that the children have to have an over-all umbrella feeling of what we're talking about and then you move in and try to work on the little things, the little subskills and what-have-you. I like the idea of having a big picture, and then seeing how we can get to that big picture. To me, that's probably the ideal. I hate the fact that the science, social studies, and health are divided up. I teach themes.

Amy: In the seventies at my school, we always taught through the integrated approach, always. We had books, we had multiple copies in books. So I taught — I didn't use any textbooks. I was never the kind of person who followed the manual. Even when I really didn't know what I was doing in the beginning, I experimented. I never read every page in a manual. I always figured things out, tried things.

Elizabeth: And I think that's the problem when some of the people don't have any renewal. All they've been taught was to use a manual and so they don't feel comfortable enough thinking on their own about what to do.

Camille: They have to *want* to learn. Same with kids, because once they have that in them, they're never going to stop [learning]. And so if you can just get them motivated internally, then half the battle is won. They need to learn to think for themselves.

Amy: But just think about how people learn. We, as adults, usually insist on knowing where we're going before we start off. We want to know what the agenda is. What's the purpose? What are we doing? We as adults can stand up and demand that, but how many times, we just piecemeal things to children. They *must* be able to construct meaning from their *total* environment. Being immersed is how they learn. It's the only thing that makes sense.

Donna: They have to be a part of their learning. They have to make decisions about what they're interested in and what they want to pursue. They have to be able to budget *their* own time and make it their classroom. So the things that are up in the room are *their* work; it's not something that *I* made and I hung up. I want them to problem solve rather than just be told, "This is what I want and this is what I want it to look like." I feel they need to work cooperatively and peer teach each other.

Mary: Yes! I like to have my kids in charge too. They have to be able to talk to each other. I think talking [sigh] is an art that sometimes is lost. They need to get into the learning spirit and know that *they're* teachers too.

Elizabeth: I'm trying to do more cooperative learning with my class and that's what I find too — that some of the kids learn better from another kid than they do from a teacher.

In-Between-the-Lines Teaching

Mary: I think flexibility is a really big key. If something happens in the school day that you need to talk about, then you should stop the so-called lesson and go into what is bothering the children. You need to go with the flow. You need to take care of that incident. Let the children talk about it. Then you can get back into the lesson. There's a lot of lessons that aren't in the books that can be taught.

Irene: Teachers can have a huge influence on kids.

Camille: I think being a teacher, you are in a leadership role. I mean, you are the leader of your classroom and you are modelling behaviors for children. Whether you're consciously doing it or whether it's just occurring, you are modelling behaviors. And kids give back what they see. You don't realize just how influential you are when you're not trying to be influential.

Donna: You have to really *know* each child.

Mary: I think you definitely have to look at the whole child. You have to look at where they're coming from, the experiences that they've had in life. . . . You have to learn what you can say to them to get them motivated. Some kids, all you have to do is look at them and they know that they need to straighten up or they need to tow the line. Some kids, you can use humor. I've used humor a lot because kids get it, they understand, and they know that they've just been put on the line [laugh], but they can laugh about it and go right on.

Amy: I use a dry sense of humor with them a lot too. It's so much nonverbal. You've *got* to learn the nonverbal cues. You can only joke with them if you know how to let them know where the limits are, and let them know what's appropriate and what isn't. Kids don't miss a whole lot and you better appreciate that if you're going to be a good teacher. You better give them a lot of credit and include them.

Elizabeth: I'm trying to put the children into a lot of situations where they're working out problems — not just for math, not just story problems — but problems about "How are you going to accomplish what needs to be accomplished?" "How about working together?" I think with children who have such great needs as far as their family backgrounds, you can't even worry about whether they're going to learn to read if they can't even learn what school is about and how you get along in a social setting. So that's one of the things I find, at this level, you've got to start them off on the track of, "How do we get along just being in a room with 25 and sharing?" While we're doing that, we're doing the stories and what-have-you, but I find that that's so important — the social aspect for the children and for their mental health: how to be a citizen and how to be a productive part of society.

Camille: Absolutely. Bill and I chose to live in Urbanville purposely because we wanted our children to have a *social* education as well as an academic education. Both of us grew up in [huge city] public schools and we didn't come out functional illiterates [laugh]. I look back on that and I think that was a real valuable experience to me because I went to school with all kinds of different people, so we wanted our children to be able to get along with people who are not exactly the same as they are.

Donna: Well, we're really talking about experiences. At school, I try to connect a lot of the things we've already done too. I do a lot of repetition with my students, like, "Oh! This is like something we did before." Connections. That's how you build your background knowledge, is by being able to connect things into it. So I'm kind of modeling for them how to build your background knowledge and retain something rather than just, "Okay, do it for this and then forget it." I want them to really build it so that they know it for their whole life. And I want them to try. I think if you want to develop risk takers, then you yourself have to be a risk taker.

Camille: To try to do the best you can. I mean, it's real easy to say, "I can't." But "I'll try" means "I'll tackle it." So I think kids need to take risks. Absolutely. Hopefully, some of these things they will develop as a part of themselves and they'll be — self-satisfaction will take care of some of it. We're trying to teach kids to be independent learners and thinkers. Working together doing collaborative projects and problem solving. I'll say to the kids when we do small group work like that, I'll say, "Well, you have to come up with X for an end product. Now, how you go about doing that is up to you. You figure out what you want to do." And they do! They go through the steps and they come up with a way to do it. I think they need to be in those kind of situations where critical thinking — all that stuff has to come through.

Amy: I think I try to model to the kids that they need to try things out too. They need to attempt things that they don't know yet. I'm always the first to say, anytime a child gives me a piece of information, I'll always say, "Well, gee! I didn't know that." Or if they ask me a question, I say, "I don't know. We're going to have to go look it up." I want them to know that there's never a point in your life when you're going to have all the answers. And I'm *not* that person, but I'm a person that can guide them to find a lot [of answers]. I *want* the children to learn from me. I want them to learn how to *think*, and I think I communicate that to them in many ways, through every lesson because I say, "You know, you *must* think through this. Don't just talk or don't just write. Let's think through this. What makes sense? What do we have to do in order to figure this out?" I think in almost everything I do, I'm trying to help them learn how to process and organize information.

Elizabeth: All the time! And a lot! Because I'm constantly [saying], "How can we work this out?" We use strategies . . . and I want the children to *find* the problem too — to create the problem and then work on it. So a lot of it is time spent on how to learn.

Mary: But I think they [children] need to see *everybody* learning and everybody teaching and everybody caring. I tell the kids I'm going to school. It's very interesting for them to see teachers go back to school. They never think of you as a learning person. I try to bring that out to the parents too, that if they're taking a course, sit down and do your homework and have your child do their homework while you're doing yours. They see that it takes effort [to go to school] and I think it also brings the teacher back to the role of being a student and how it feels. There's so much for them to learn . . . I really try to make each child feel that they can make it.

Adjusting Curriculum to Contexts

Elizabeth: It's great to have people who keep stressing that the needs of the children have to come before the materials or the curriculum. The kids are the most important, and the curriculum — of course, we're supposed to teach it and we *try* to get those things across. But we can add and subtract within that curriculum and meet kids' needs. I find that we're presented with materials, but the idea is, you don't teach materials, you teach children. So I use the materials that I find worthwhile. I don't use the parts that I don't think are worthwhile, no matter whether the school system bought them or not. If I don't find it a way to work with *kids*, I don't use it. I'll try to make or find my own — whatever's going to work — or have the children create it.

Mary: Or get it from other teachers. I'm not happy with my whole language program right now. Well, our school had this young man coming in with whole language experience and I thought to myself, "I can learn from this person." I didn't think to myself, "He's going to be a better teacher than I am" or "I need to cut him off at the pass." [laugh] I don't see it that way. I always look for the learning end. I can learn from any teacher. I've always — I always want to learn something new. I like to try new things. If someone tells me there's a better way to teach, I'll be the first one to try it. And then I usually adapt it to my teaching style, so it isn't exactly like the other person's, but it's — you have to absorb it in and then put it out in a way that you can teach. I do it in a way that I feel I can use it in my classroom.

Elizabeth: I appreciate that and I *love* to see that kind of thing: something new; something a little different; a new slant on things; look and see how other people do things — "Oh! Okay. There's a new way." It's helpful, it really is. It makes your year, your day, your hour, every bit of it go better when you can find some other approach, an alternative . . .

Irene: Exactly. Different people have different ways of learning. So because a child learns by language experience doesn't mean this child isn't going to learn by phonics. So I do the big books and I do the beginning sounds and I do the letter recognition and I still have those old basals that we were told to burn. So what if they want to take it home and show off what they can read because the vocabulary is controlled. Why not give them a book that they can read and feel successful with, even though I hate the stories. And it's not like all they're getting is this book because they're getting an environment of rich literature too.

Amy: I'm still forced into doing many things I don't want to do. I do them — my own way — but I do them. And there are things I *must* do and I've had to learn: Yeah, I still have to give standardized tests and it makes my skin turn cold. But I've also learned how to prepare my students how to take them so it's not such a horrible aggravation to them. There are ways to prepare them to take tests like that without it blowing them out of the water. When I started to see learning as continual growth, continual process, I started giving projects that were very open-ended and I just let them go with it. I felt very confused at the time. I knew I was heading in the right direction, but I didn't . . . I felt it was too loose. I knew that I needed to be doing something different but I didn't have enough knowledge base behind me to really judge what I was seeing. Then I started really doing a lot of reading, and talking to very knowledgeable people, and putting those pieces together. I know why I'm trying things now. And I know how to tell when they don't have the background for something. I know the necessity of building that background now, a lot more than I ever did before. I don't ever think I really thought that much about prior knowledge in building background before. I'm still working on it.

Camille: And as a teacher, I need the background knowledge too. I have to do a lot of reading, or finding out, or sometimes talking to people. Asking an expert in the field or "How would you go about doing this?" or talking to colleagues and saying, "Have you ever taught X? What did you do? What worked for you?" So I think all those things are real valuable for the teacher. You're required, as far as teaching goes, to teach from a course of study and so you need to be aware of what those things are and cover them in the best way that you can so that the kids are exposed to as many things as you can fit into the number of days of school. [laugh] In fact, through all my years, the best way I found to deal with a course of study is, I decide what it is I'm going to teach. I know the major topics in the course of study. I teach unit-wise and I teach integrated. So I pick a theme or a topic and then I do as many things with that theme as I can come up with, and then I go to my course of study and say, "I did this, I did this, I did this." At the end, if there's something I haven't covered, I'll make a special attempt to go over that, but it's much easier to do it that way for *me* because with all of my different activities, I cover a lot of that course of study and more. Rather than to go through that book one by one and say, "Well, today I'm going to do this and Tomorrow I'm going to do that." Because that has *no* continuity for kids and it doesn't show them how to make links; it doesn't show them how it relates to life. But if you take a topic and do as many things with that topic as you can come up with so the kids really are involved, you cover all of that course of study stuff. I do try to connect for kids and show them how to make connections for themselves.

Donna: Sure. From day to day and year to year, as the students change, so does my focus, my curriculum. Of course, you have your overall course of study which confines you to that, but there's ways to manipulate that into being more appropriate for the group of students you have. And I've changed every year. I throw out my lesson plans from the year before. I am not a teacher who looks back. I just find myself more enthusiastic or more fresh if I start over fresh every year and don't look back and see what I did last year. It's to keep me revitalized and ready to go. As well as, every year you know, there's new things that should — that come up and can be done. I would hate to be so confined to what I did the year before and miss a perfect event.

Irene: I *cannot* [laugh] — my favorite units, I'll do again, but I do not copy anything exactly. I *never* do anything exactly the same way.

Camille: I don't think, even though I have the same grade, that I ever do the same lesson twice the same way. I have an interest in children's books — I'm always at the bookstore looking for new books, new ways to come across with information, things that have to be covered in the course of study — partly for me, because it makes it interesting for me. I have a real hard time doing the same thing over and over again. I'd much rather find a whole new way to do it. That's one of the wonderful things about children's literature: There's so many new books that are always coming out and there's always a new approach to something.

Adjusting Assessment to Beliefs about Learning
Donna: Like the new approach to assessment! I'm excited about alternative assessment. I truly *believe* in it. I think at first, people are intimidated

by it because it's a change from the norm and that change can sometimes be very frightening, but it's going to benefit them and the kids so much more.

Amy: I don't slot growth. Most of the things I really care about in reading and writing aren't measurable. It's just a continual growth. I believe in having objectives for what you want the children to learn and grow towards, but there's this continuum of growth throughout every objective. There's not a, "Well, you've got this if you can answer these four questions."

Elizabeth: I get a little concerned when it's strictly a report card. I really like to do things [with] a portfolio approach where I can make note of a child's breakthrough.

Amy: I *love* using portfolios during [parent/teacher] conferences. That eases the tension. I would much rather show a portfolio than defend a grade. I hate grades with a passion. I spent last summer creating 'writing prompts' [on a committee] for assessment purposes — tried to make them so instructionally pure that teachers can learn process from these prompts. We see assessment as being totally linked with instruction, so these prompts are instructional for students as well as teachers.

Mary: Justifying it and going beyond just pencil and paper kinds of things.

Elizabeth: Today, I wrote down on my little notes, "Henry actually used a strategy — recognized a word, went back, and self-corrected." So he was monitoring. I'd like to be able to point that kind of thing out [to parents]. To me, that's the true evaluation of the child — not just the tests. Likewise if you see they're *not* making any progress. I have one little boy and he is at the top of the group. But I can see he's made no growth. He's there, and he's just staying there whereas some of the kids who are the very lowest are beginning to build up some strategies. I feel better about them, even though they're far behind him, than I do about the one who knows a lot of words and never extends himself. Learning is lifelong. You start somewhere and you've got to keep going. You always have to be doing something — reading, or getting better, or trying it, or finding out from someone else.

Camille: I piloted an alternative reading assessment instrument and it's not a typical standardized test; it's open-ended. And it's not multiple choice.

I'm really not a multiple choice person at all 'cause kids guess, and they often don't understand what they're doing.

Amy: Exactly. I think what I'm assessing my children on now is not — I'm not so much worried about their reading level anymore as I truly understand that what they read has so much to do with what they're bringing to that particular reading experience. Again, you're talking prior knowledge, plus motivation . . . I just don't take "no" for an answer when I'm really challenging them. But only if it's a thing that I know they can handle. If it's just because it's hard work — a lot of learning is very hard work. I want them to get used to — that it's fun, it's hard work, and when you're done, you feel great about it — that "fun" isn't always to sit back and let it flow over you and just happen to you. Fun is being involved and making your mind go round and producing something you're proud of. When they're finished, they're really *proud*.

Teaching Beyond the Classroom
Irene: As I assess my children, I make notes of what I need to instruct the parents to do at home. You know, little things they can do to help.

Mary: Indispensable. In fact, the first year I came over to Cherryhill School, I had a parent group whom I met with. I said, "What do you want me to do in this second grade? What do you feel is important?" Because I think it's important children know that the parent is there, [that] they know that the parent is working with and involved with the teacher. I try to make them feel like a partner, a part of the child's work. I don't ever talk down to them. I try to find out a little bit about them and I bring it on a level of we're just friends chatting over the coffee table. I want them to feel that they're able to talk to me about something. If they're having frustrations about how to deal with a child's behavior, I'll give them some of my suggestions. I try to give them concrete things — things that they can do. And I *always* try to keep them informed through my weekly reports.

Elizabeth: Or on curriculum nights [in September]. "This is what I expect. This is what is expected of a first grader. By the end of the year, he better be able to do this and this, so we *have* to work together. You've got to help me. You've got to let me know when you're not able to work on it or when you don't understand."

Camille: Early in September, I ask the parents to tell me about the strengths and weaknesses of their child and I also give parents a little questionnaire asking what areas they would like me to focus in on with their child. You know, I give them an opportunity to let me know what areas they want me to zero in on because they know their child at the beginning better than I do. So I try to work *very* closely with my parents and I think I've been real successful with that. They [other teachers] tease me at school because I always have a crowd in my room every day after school or observing during the day. I think it's real important to cultivate a relationship so that they know I am approachable and available. I tell them right from the get-go at the beginning [of the year], "Don't worry about calling me. If you have something on your mind, please call, please come in, send a note because I need to know what you're thinking and I need us to interact." So, I work real hard to make my parents feel that I am accessible and I *want* to be accessible so that if I need to go to them for a concern, that I will be well received. I think parents need to be told that they are needed and welcomed, and there are all kinds of things we can do together.

Donna: You're lucky to have parents with phones. I start with a note. As a matter of fact, I've had to use tape recordings before, rather than notes. We had a tape recorder that we would send home with oral notes on it rather than written because parents didn't read or write. It worked out really well. If the note doesn't make it home, I make a phone call. If they don't have a phone, that's about when I need to make a home visit. So it's a challenge and it's a lot of work, and it gets tiresome after awhile to not be able to have that immediate home contact. So you have to work hard at it and it takes a lot of time away from what I'd rather be doing . . .

Elizabeth: But they [parents] have to be a part of it, so it's real important that they understand. You need their cooperation 'cause you can't do it alone. I think some parents still feel it's the school's job to do everything, but I think some of them would like to help if they knew what to do — if they had some ideas. I have three who have asked for homework [for first graders]. I said, "Well, we don't usually do homework, but the homework is this, this, and this." Then I sent home some little flashcards and a couple of the kids came back with them dog-eared, so I know they were working. Parents who haven't had any training tend to think that's the best way they can help. And I don't care; if they show the child they believe in it, then the kid's going to want to do it. I know all the talk about "Don't give them a flashcard," but if it works for that parent — if that child sees that Mom's interested, then they're going to want to do what they need to do for school.

Discussion

In a study of exemplary teachers, Campbell (1988) found that exemplary teachers have a view of teaching and children that is holistic in nature and that "[w]ork, play, and concern for an interest in the continuing growth of self, family, friends, students, and peers — humanity in general — overlapped and became the integrated, integral, and dominating ethic of these expert teachers" (p. 50). This study corroborated his work: Learning for themselves and others is of paramount, ongoing importance to the participants. Throughout the interviews, I was constantly amazed at the centrality of their beliefs to everything they do.

What are the strong beliefs these teachers hold? The participants have not always held these beliefs exactly as they are at this point in their career; their beliefs continue to evolve and to be refined. Their conceptualization of teaching/learning includes common, guiding beliefs that:

1. all children can learn and that it is the responsibility of the teacher to try various techniques and approaches to find out what will work for each child;
2. children do not all learn in the same ways since each is a unique individual;
3. a holistic approach to teaching improves learning;
4. knowledge is constructed, so care is taken in uncovering prior knowledge and building on it;
5. children, as learners, are teachers; teachers must also be learners;
6. teachers need to know each child very well in order to assist their intellectual, social, and emotional development;
7. genuine understanding (Gardner, 1991) or generative knowledge (Resnick and Klopfer, 1989) is a high priority, so continuity and connections in learning are emphasized;
8. teaching is guided by the child's strengths and interests;
9. learning is a continuous process, a "continuum of growth";
10. self-reliance and independence of students is the ultimate goal;
11. time must be spent teaching children how to learn (learning about learning);
12. involvement of parents as teachers is crucial to learning (This includes learning from parents as well as "teaching" and communicating with parents.);

13. learning requires risk taking and mistakes. How the consequences of risks and failures are handled is also important learning.

Linked to these beliefs is a set of ideals (behaviors, values, dispositions) these teachers "teach," largely through modelling. I have referred to them as in-between-the-lines teaching. They include problem finding, problem solving, risk taking, flexibility, respect for others, decision making skills, positive conflict resolution, doing one's best, satisfaction and pride associated with effort and work, and continuous learning. Many of these same dispositions and ethics were mentioned in the teachers' stories about what they learned in their own childhood.

These articulated beliefs directly influence how the teachers approach the explicit curriculum. As Mary explained, "You have to absorb [a new idea] in and then put it out in a way that you can teach. I do it in a way that I feel I can use it in my classroom." Willing and eager to try new ideas and possibilities, these teachers carefully consider how those ideas will improve teaching/learning and how they fit into existing beliefs about teaching/learning. Not only is self-knowledge necessary (articulation of beliefs), but reflection and further inquiry also play a key role in improving their practice. I submit that this process is vital as a form of renewal and as a way to improve teaching; it is teaching and learning combined.

The teachers have never felt bound to follow a manual; rather, they "add and subtract within that curriculum" using what works with a given group of students or what they judge to be worthwhile. Sometimes, when their beliefs about teaching/learning clash with the principal's or district's directives, they alter curriculum in order to retain congruency between their beliefs and practices. One possible explanation for "curriculum sabotage" by teachers may have to do with whether the innovation fits into the teacher's belief system. For example, several of the participants believe strongly that holistic learning is better than fragmented learning, so they continue to teach using integrated and thematic units despite the district's insistence on separate subject areas.

The self-renewal the participants engage in is strongly influenced by their own belief that an effective teacher must be a learner and by their work ethic: that if you care about something, you learn "to make it better". So they are constantly looking for alternatives that work better and thus look upon everything and everyone as a potential resource toward improving teaching and learning. They are very innovative when it comes to communicating with parents, finding ways to have parents contribute to their children's learning, and soliciting the knowledge of parents concerning the strengths and weaknesses of their children. In fact, teaching beyond the classroom, whether it involves newsletters, telephone calls, anecdotal report cards, curriculum presentations to parents, or scouring the public library for books, occupies a great deal of these teachers' time. The importance they place on human interactions and continuous learning (for themselves and others) is underscored in their beliefs and resulting decisions concerning teaching and learning.

Personal and Professional Renewal

The self . . . in continuous formation through choice of action.
Dewey (1916/1966, p. 351)

Research question: How do exemplary teachers self-renew personally and professionally?

Personal Renewal

Five of the participants indicated numerous outlets for relaxation and personal enjoyment. For example, Mary paints, is a soloist, loves watching football games, and relaxes on a boat while Elizabeth travels, goes to movies, and enjoys theater and concert performances, reading, and baking. Camille has season's tickets to the symphony, ballet, and live theater. She also enjoys reading, as do Amy and Donna who are involved in sports or athletics. In addition to spending time with their families, these five are all active in the community in various ways as well: from serving in a church or temple to fundraising for a community scholarship; from membership in the PTA (Parent/Teacher Association) to participation in the Historical Society; and from helping the Cancer Society to collecting for the United Way.

Even though the teachers mentioned that personal renewal is important in keeping their perspective in life or helping them remain enthusiastic and tolerant at work, they do not necessarily separate their personal renewal from their professional life.

I think that you need a break from school every once in awhile. Teaching being the twenty-four hour job that it is, you're never caught up. So it's very relaxing for me to sit at the symphony or to sit at the ballet. But while I'm doing that — I mean, I can't tell you how many times I've come up with a bulletin board idea or a writing project at the symphony, because when you're sitting there, your mind just — you know, sometimes you're trying to think of something and there you are and it's a very soothing place to sit and ideas spring into your head. So lots of times, I've come up with ideas sitting in the theater [laugh]. (Camille)

The personal renewal? Oh gosh! It makes me have a whole new outlook. It renews me to go back there [an inner city school] and try my best because those kids *don't* go home at night thinking — or at least, maybe they do even

think that their life is okay, but an *outsider* is not looking at their life thinking that it's okay. So I go in and give it my best shot. For their sake. They
need it, they deserve it. They've got a lot rougher life than any of us have
ever had. I'm willing to give them 110% because they deserve it. (Donna)

Irene did not mention any hobbies or community service in which she participates.
Apart from her time at school, she spends her energy being with her family and her
parents and siblings, although she doesn't spend as much time with them as she
would like to now that she teaches full time. Like the other teachers, her personal
and professional lives often merge: She finds herself thumbing through a school
magazine while waiting for her child's piano lesson to end or thinking about possibilities for a musical production while looking at catalogues.

Professional Renewal

*Neither policy makers nor researchers have devoted much attention to
learning how teachers add to their own knowledge of a field, or to chart-
ing the paths by which advances in the disciplines come to the attention of
teachers.*

Little (1992b, p. 188)

Although professional development and staff development are frequently used
terms in education, they are often conceptualized as professional activities generally initiated by an organization for a group of teachers and conducted at a pre-
selected site and time (Barnes and Putnam, 1981). What the data from this study
show, however, is that much of teachers' professional renewal goes far beyond such
a limited definition and that a great deal is job-embedded or engaged in privately
(individually or with a few colleagues) out of school.

The teachers view their renewal holistically. For example, reading may be assigned by a university professor for a graduate course, but a teacher may spot a
familiar name in the references and seek out the article because of personal interest.
Similarly, it may be the private reflection following an inservice presentation that
yields the deepest insights, or the conversation during coffee break that is most
helpful. This overlap may contribute to the difficulty of uncovering just how teachers engage in professional renewal.

To prompt discussion of their professional renewal, the participants referred to a
list of possible professional development activities compiled from a focus group
interview with veteran teachers and from the literature (Appendix C). None of the
teachers has been in the position of clinical faculty member although Irene and
Elizabeth applied to specific schools in the hope that the schools would be selected
as Professional Development Schools. Amy and Camille were disappointed that

their schools submitted a proposal to become a Professional Development School, but were not selected.

Nor has any participant written for publication although three expressed interest. Camille kept the journals her kindergarten class wrote between September and June so that she can write an article for other teachers, but she has not yet found time. As for the other possibilities on the list, one or more of the teachers has engaged in each of the other activities. Additionally, the participants added to the list the activities of: team leader; being designated "in charge" during a principal's absence; member of the district's negotiating team; union positions; staff retreats; home visits; delegate to state or national educational meetings; and organizer for a conference.

When analyzing the teachers' renewal using the expanded definition described by Howey (1985), it appears that the participants have undertaken activities that could lead to development in each area. However, most of their renewal seems to have been engaged in for pedagogical development, understanding of self and others, and career development. A member check confirmed that the teachers perceive that they also engage in professional activities that have the potential to enhance theoretical and cognitive development. Mentioned particularly as activities that really stretched their thinking and knowledge were district teams to write curriculum and examine alternative assessments, as well as leadership roles as district resource persons. The participants believe that reflection is very important to their growth. All of the teachers perceive their knowledge of or experience with research and inquiry to be under-represented compared to the other five areas, although they believe that many activities hold the potential to encourage growth in several areas at the same time. In other words, their own learning appears to be holistic in the same way they perceive their students' learning as holistic.

Renewal and social interaction

What is noteworthy in listening to the teachers discuss their renewal is that most of their renewal comes through social interactions; it is the human contact that is remembered. Amy took a university class to deepen her understanding of how children learn to read, but found a different kind of renewal at the same time.

My thinking was *totally* stimulated because of this group of women I was with. We were all veteran teachers and we were all in the classroom at the time. It was that relationship I had with the class that was excellent.

Donna enjoyed going out to eat with a colleague after a graduate class and the stimulating conversations that resulted. Mary met two new colleagues through an inservice workshop and began to exchange ideas with them. "So now we write letters back and forth and I send little things through the mail to them if I find something really neat."

Camille talked about the collegial friends she made in graduate school and still sees. It was also there that she began to subscribe personally to professional journals and to join professional organizations.

> I continue my memberships because I think it's good to be professionally active and to get current materials and to find out what's happening across the country. During the school year, it's very hard to find the time to read professional things. I certainly don't read them in depth the way I wish I had the time to do. But on the other hand, I know what's current and I like to see who the articles are written by and where this research is being done.

She considers discussions at meetings of professional organizations or in journals "a different level of conversation [but] I also need to have conversations with people so I can learn from them."

The teachers frequently talk with colleagues to get second opinions, to hear alternative solutions, to share ideas and information, and to seek support.

> Lots of times, we ask each other for advice with a particular kid. Like, if I have a kid that somebody else had last year, I'll go to that teacher and say, "What did you do with [that student]? How did you get him to do this?" Or with a parent where there is a difficulty, "How did you work with that parent? Can you give me some suggestions?" So I think going to other teachers and other people, even community people, and asking for advice is a very valid and useful way of getting information. (Camille)

> I worked on a summer writing team and I met a wide variety of teachers from all over the system, which — we all shared lots of stories, unrelated to what we were supposed to be working on, but shared lots of stories about how to run a classroom and how to make it better; what new resources were out there for us to obtain and use; and it also gave me some experience in seeing other aspects of what education is all about. (Donna)

> I think it helps your self-worth to know other people out there value you, value your work. You can go to [another teacher] and say, "I had a terrible day" and no one but a teacher would know how terrible some days can be. . . I think we know the problems and sometimes we know that we can't solve them, and just having that to share and someone saying, "Well you know, I had that same situation happen to me and you handled it well" or "You've

done all you can." That kind of support is what you really and truly need. (Mary)

In addition to conversations, observing other teachers, and being observed by others (discussed earlier), two additional sources of renewal were mentioned as being exceedingly beneficial: reflection and reading recovery training.

Reflection

All of the participants talked about the importance of reflection in order to improve their practice. Amy explained that she has always been a writer "to keep my sanity" while Donna and Camille have had some experience with journal writing in graduate school and in reading recovery training. They have also had their students write as a result. However, most of their own reflection now is not written.

> I think we're always evaluating ourself. My mind is constantly on that kind of stuff and you're always looking for a better way to do something or a new way to do something. And sometimes, when something doesn't work — and that happens a lot! [laugh] —you have to sit down and say, "Well, what was wrong with this? Why didn't it work? Was it an inappropriate time? Were these kids not ready to do this or was there a discipline problem that became too much of a problem?" So I think constantly, in every free moment, your mind is thinking about those kinds of things. . . . In one class that I took in graduate school, we had to have a reflective journal, a response to the class and our readings. At first it sounded awful and laborious, but what it did was, it made you conscious of your thoughts. I found it real informative because it made me think how I relate what I read to what I do every day and how my time in those classes related to what I read and what I was doing. I do it with my kids when they finish a book or when we finish a unit — to let me know what they liked, what they learned, just their own impression on what you're giving and how they like it. It's feedback — that's exactly what it is — and I find that real helpful. (Camille)

> I do tend to reflect at the end of the day when I get home. Then I have time to think about, "Ah, that didn't work [laugh]. I'm going to try something different tomorrow." More or less, I think about: How did things go with the children? How did it work? What do I need to do to make it better the next day? I do a lot of looking at the materials I'm using to see how they're being used by the kids: Are they enjoying them? — especially books, things that I make, and what-have-you. Are they being used? Are they able to read them? Do I need more? Maybe I didn't introduce it right. Do I need to

make a chart with it? I do a lot of that kind of thing. It is internal reflection. (Elizabeth)

Reading recovery training

Elizabeth, Camille, and Donna place enormous value on the experiences they had in reading recovery as well as the wide network of close colleagues that resulted from teaching and learning together as a group over an extended time. Theory, practice, observation, feedback, and reflection are components of the training. But there were other outcomes for the teachers as well: exposure to professional knowledge and a new vocabulary that allowed thinking, understanding, teaching, and discussion at a new level.

> I wouldn't give up my reading recovery training for anything. I think it was the best learning that I was provided. It gave me the *discipline* to do reading in a more beneficial way. I didn't just depend on a teacher's manual anymore. As a matter of fact, I don't even use teacher's manuals. What I use is outside professional literature that I read, articles that I read. . . (Donna)

> I think that I learned more in my year's training in reading recovery than in all the education I had prior to that. Plus, what it did was, it gave you a vocabulary. All the techniques you did — I mean, when you taught children to read, you did a lot of what reading recovery does. But you didn't necessarily have the terminology and you couldn't explain it to a parent. You couldn't say, "This is directionality. This is integrating the cue system." Reading recovery gave a teacher terminology to communicate what they're doing with the students and with the teachers. I think that, for me, that was a very, very significant thing. I think it gives you confidence. And it also gives specific things for parents to look at: "Was your child doing this? Is your child doing that?" Otherwise, before, it was, "Is your child reading?" Well, there's a lot to reading! What are the things that need to be done? It [reading recovery] breaks down very clearly what the child can do; what the child needs to learn to do. (Elizabeth)

> As far as the knowledge base that you get, it's wonderful. You learn about strategies, and you learn how to teach children things, and you learn . . . I guess when I started teaching [and] I took all these reading courses, I knew what I was doing, but I don't think I had vocabulary. I didn't have language to explain every single thing I was doing. I knew what to do and I did it. Reading recovery provides the language. You can use that language to explain to a parent, you can explain it to the other children, you can explain it

to an administrator, you can explain it to other teachers. It teaches you how to make people aware of everything you do when you learn to read. To me, that's invaluable. (Camille)

It is interesting to note that the same outcomes occurred when Amy, who had not had reading recovery training, was selected for a resource leadership role at the district level.

That [job] was my education, probably the best one I ever received. Then I started really doing a lot of reading, and talking to very knowledgeable people, and putting those pieces together, and felt very good about that. I know *why* I'm trying things now. [laugh] That helps. I got into the whole philosophy of the thing and learned to put all these wonderful words with what I had been doing, but I didn't have all the right labels for. It was great! I loved it!

Scope of involvement

Research question: Is there an expanding scope of professional awareness, involvement, and contribution throughout their career? (e.g., classroom, school, district, state, national, international)

All of the teachers mentioned the importance of observing other grade levels or of changing grades in order to get an understanding and overview of the curriculum across the grades. At the school level, Mary believes it helps teachers to know the policies and procedures of the district so they can better understand the decisions taken at the individual school level. Donna saw her team work to create a school focus as an important factor in developing a sense of involvement beyond the classroom. Although all got involved in school committees early in their careers, it was not until they started attending district meetings and workshops or graduate school that they began to build a collegial network beyond the school. As their involvement broadened, their network grew and it was through the network that they were invited to participate on district level committees.

The teachers recognize the importance of committee work at the district level.

It gives you the behind-the-scenes of your job. Without that behind-the-scenes, you don't know why you got that memo in your mailbox telling you to do something. You don't know why everyone in the building is talking about this focus. Well, they're talking about it because a committee is implementing something new. If you're just in your room and you're only working with your students, you just don't see that unless you get involved in stuff. Plus you appreciate the amount of time that people put in. It does take time. And people that are already at a stage beyond a beginning teacher, they need that chance to shine on a committee and to show what they can offer. (Donna)

Camille mentioned how helpful it was for her to hear various perspectives from a committee that included elementary, middle school, and high school teachers from many schools. Five teachers talked about joining committees as a way of being involved, learning a lot, and making a difference. But several were quick to point out that it is important that they believe in what the committee is working on, such as promotion and retention or alternative assessments, and want to see changes in current practice. Frequently, district committee work led to further career development such as presenting at workshops or conferences, piloting programs, or participating on an interview team. Being a resource person for the district was also considered to be a similar, wonderful experience.

All of the participants belong to professional organizations and/or personally subscribe to educational magazines and journals. This gives them the opportunity to find out what is happening locally or nationally and sometimes internationally. They seem to have relied on graduate school, reading recovery training, or their network to find professional reading. The same was true for finding out about conferences.

Donna began attending conferences as a student teacher. She has continued to enjoy them and to seek further opportunities to attend. Of the four veteran teachers who now have experience attending and/or presenting at state, national, or international conferences or meetings, all were quite far into their careers before having the opportunity to attend their first conference outside of the district. As Amy put it, "I'm now hooked." Conferences may help them to understand various roles in the educational enterprize, be they teacher, researcher, teacher educator, the union, or publishers. It may also be a way to encourage teachers to be producers of knowledge and to offer an avenue for sharing their knowledge with a wider audience of colleagues.

I attended the IRA (International Reading Association) conference and that was marvelous fun, but I haven't presented there. But now that I've gone, I know I could. At first, I thought, "Well, this is the nation. This is the world! This is international. Who do I think I am?" And then I went to hear a few people and I thought, "Well gee . . ." [laugh] and it does your ego a world of good. Now, there were obviously people there talking about things that I had plenty to learn from. But there were plenty talking that were on the level I was on. (Amy)

Donna has enjoyed a very different socialization process from the others and, through a variety of experiences, gained a global perspective very early in her career. For the other five teachers, there was a definite but slower progression of involvement, interest, and contribution beginning with the classroom and then, to differing degrees, extending to the school, district, state, nation, and world. All have contributed personal time and money for their renewal, but are indebted to their collegial network for helping them grow.

From very early in their careers, the participants were involved in situations that encouraged them to seek knowledge beyond themselves and to work with other adults whose support they came to value. Open space schools, team teaching, observation with honest analysis and feedback, specialized training, school committees, graduate school — all of these encouraged the teachers to search outward. Their scope expanded to include meaningful involvement and relationships at the district level and beyond through professional organizations, journals, committees, conferences, and leadership roles. In one form or another, they all saw expanding understanding of the educational enterprize as part of their definition of professionalism (also see Berman, 1987; Campbell, 1988; and Leithwood, 1990). This expanding scope has allowed them to relate their work to a larger context.

What I am suggesting is that these teachers sought an ever-broadening scope of involvement in an attempt to understand more thoroughly what they deeply care about, namely education. They also sought — and continue to seek — involvement (a habit established before becoming teachers) for personal satisfaction, as learning opportunities, and as a means of influencing decisions affecting their work. Involvement is only a means to an end; the goal is to improve teaching/learning for their students and themselves. Active participation in their own education has helped them shift from external motivation to intrinsic motivation, the same shift they seek to effect in their own students.

The teachers' widening scope of involvement has also shaped and refined their beliefs about teaching and learning. Although some started their career with a strong image of a teacher (an image that included learning and caring about others), their beliefs have evolved and been refined, largely through practical knowledge. Learning professional vocabulary and discovering that others in the educational arena hold similar beliefs has greatly increased their confidence.

Their involvement and increased confidence is gratifying to them, much like that of veteran teachers in a study by Yee (1990). She concluded that veteran teachers who have decided to make teaching a career value professional growth opportunities and challenges that include "collegial exchange, opportunities to take on additional roles and to participate in decisions. . . . They want to exercise some control over what matters most to them — student learning" (pp. 114-115). To influence decisions, the teachers in this study volunteered for positions on district committees and willingly participated on writing teams, increasing yet again their knowledge and collegial network (also see Little, 1992a). Like ripples on a pond, their increasing scope of involvement is similar to the circle described by Yee (1990) and Rosenholtz (1989): Highly committed teachers more actively seek growth opportunities, as do teachers whose workplace conditions generate satisfying intrinsic rewards (Yee, 1990); what they learn increases their sense of efficacy and teacher certainty which, in turn, encourages further renewal (Rosenholtz, 1989). When a sense of efficacy and intrinsic rewards are both high, teachers tend to stay in teaching (Yee, 1990, p. 115). This suggests that broadening teachers' scope of awareness of and involvement in the educational community may increase teacher commitment to education.

A credibility gap

All six participants mentioned a "credibility gap" preventing or limiting respect of teacher leaders and sometimes interfering with their own learning. What they were referring to goes hand in hand with the theory/practice gap: They want teacher educators and resource leaders to be able to work through the many steps required to link theory or district goal statements with practice. Elizabeth has been on both sides of the issue. As a resource leader, she was asked to give inservice sessions to teachers to implement a new reading series. "I'd say, 'Oh, my gosh, I've never used this series. I've never taught that and here I am telling her [another teacher] what she'd better do.' Teachers tend to resent that very much."

Amy, who also has had a term appointment as a resource leader, shares Elizabeth's impression that when term limits are not applied to teacher leader positions, people either seek alternative roles to avoid the classroom or, once out of the classroom, are afraid to go back. Amy claims that "it's true with resource [personnel], supervisors, *and* principals. Too many are out there because they don't want to deal with the classroom. And those people can not tell a classroom teacher how to do it. Unless you've lived it, you don't know it. You know some pie-in-the-sky kinds of things but people are pie-in-theskied to death. Don't tell me just to integrate my curriculum, don't tell me to flexible group — I don't know *how*."

As a veteran teacher trying to implement whole language, Mary read and experimented with different possibilities, but still felt her program was not flowing smoothly. She recognized that she needed to see a skilled teacher in action and have an opportunity to discuss details with that teacher. Instead, all she got was another inservice session with the district resource person. "She's not credible to me 'cause she has not been in the classroom for ages and has not taught with this program. She's not taught a whole language classroom. So, to me, it would be useless to hear her because in my mind, I'd be shutting her off because she has not dealt with it."

For the same reason, three of the teachers did not spare professors, even though they respected them as persons. Said Irene, "The professors were wonderful people, they had great ideas, but they had no practical experience in the classroom." This credibility gap does not seem to be disrespect on the part of the teachers, but rather, a genuine need to synthesize professional and practical knowledge and frustration with not being able to achieve it, especially when they recognize its potential for helping improve teaching and learning.

Discussion

The participants have an openness to learning, a willingness to believe that learning can take place anywhere and from a myriad of possible resources. School walls may exist, but they do not stop these teachers from drawing on students, colleagues, parents, the community, and beyond for resources and information. In no way do the participants limit the boundaries of learning to institutions or think that their learning will ever be complete. On the contrary, they are delighted that learning does not end: They keep interest and fun in their own learning by constantly seeking new ideas and approaches.

The teachers' personal renewal, as well as their wider community and professional contacts, help them keep their work in perspective. With the exception of Irene, whose personal interest focusses primarily on her family, the participants' interests and involvement are so broad and varied that if one area does not go well, enjoyment or success in other areas can compensate for or at least minimize a difficulty or "flop" at school. They rely heavily on collegial support during traumatic personal experiences. Collegial networks have also played an important role in the professional renewal of all six participants, particularly in moving their professional scope of interest and involvement beyond the school level.

Huberman (1993) wrote about elementary teachers' "isolation in an infantilized environment, in which teachers can roam no further, intellectually speaking, than the brightest of their pupils" (p. 31). Quite unlike this picture, the participants spend a great deal of time with adults outside the classroom. They enjoy many different kinds of adult collegial relationships which contribute to their learning. Again, for them, learning and human interaction are intertwined.

The participants also use their time in the classroom to learn about and from their students. They are fascinated with the development of children and use any opportunity to learn from them. What they observe and theorize about in the classroom concerning children's development and learning forms a basis for the professional renewal they undertake outside the classroom.

When the participants began to teach, they engaged in professional renewal immediately. All mentioned that professional conversations, reflection, experimentation, reading, and working with parent volunteers occurred at the beginning of their careers. Two unusual early-career activities included involvement in a Teachers' Center and belonging to a teacherinitiated group that met on Saturdays to share ideas and make instructional materials.

Most of the participants did not get into the habit of attending conferences until late (15-20 years) into their career. Other kinds of renewal beyond their school tended to occur in the second decade of the teachers' careers. Since the scope of renewal depended so heavily on collegial networks, it may be that it took them that long to build up a wide network and become known in their district.

The exception is Donna who was invited to conduct workshops and participate on committees, writing teams, and interview teams at the district level within the first six years of her career. Thanks to her first principal, Donna had been given professional opportunities at the school level during her first and second year of teaching. Additionally, she started her Master's program immediately, as well as reading recovery training. Both gave her a wide collegial network from which she was frequently suggested for various new opportunities.

The only participant to have a mentor was Amy when she was selected for a resource leadership role. That relationship had a powerful and positive effect on her search for more and deeper renewal. She recognized the need to read for background knowledge and philosophy so she could explain district policy to her colleagues. For the first time, she attended conferences, thus becoming interested and involved at the national and international level. With the exception of Donna's first principal, principals did not play a major role in the participants' renewal.

The area of research and inquiry, including an understanding of how to interpret and apply it, is problematic for the participants: They perceive this area of renewal to be the one in which they have the least knowledge and experience. As Little (1987) noted, there are few mechanisms in schools to promote research by teachers (pp. 502-503). The teachers in this study would be very interested in learning about and participating in research, but seem to have little idea how to tap this source of renewal even though they grasp the excitement and potential it could offer at this stage in their career.

The participants talked about various levels of conversation they have with different groups of colleagues. Unlike the teachers in Jackson's (1968/1990) study, these participants were able to identify and articulate their beliefs and give carefully supported evidence for curricular decisions. My impression was that much of the renewal they sought, particularly theoretical development, was specifically undertaken in order to find explanations and support for their practices. The teachers tend to rely on discussions with colleagues and experimentation (sometimes painful) in their classrooms in order to link practice with theory or their own theorizing. The teachers were unanimous in their opinion that only people with recent and considerable classroom experience have enough credibility to help them with this difficult task.

Where the participants perceived themselves to have "really been stretched" was in experiences such as reading recovery training (over the course of a year) and on curricular writing teams (over several summers or an extended period of time) with other stimulating colleagues in the district. Not only was the work exciting for them, but the collegial relationships were rewarding and close. Also, the exhilarating, liberating confidence the teachers got from specialized knowledge and its accompanying vocabulary cannot be underestimated .

This suggests that the work of small groups of teachers, spending prolonged time examining an area that is meaningful to their practice, can be an exciting form of renewal — a form of inquiry. Additionally, this form of renewal acknowledges teachers' ability to contribute to and influence work they consider meaningful and important: teaching and learning. This kind of "teacher discussion" renewal, even if guided by a tactful "expert," might also go a long way toward avoiding the credibility gap that seems to impede their learning.

Factors Enabling and/or Constraining Renewal

Research Questions: Which personal and contextual factors enable and/or constrain exemplary teachers' renewal? How do they deal with constraints on their renewal?

The guided interview schedule (Appendix B) suggested nine areas of discussion that could be related to organizational factors enabling and/or constraining teachers' renewal. Without fail, the teachers selected only the following factors: collegiality, the principal, district support, and resources. However, also important to them (and unanticipated by me) were issues of professionalism, respect, power, and school transfers. Because the participants see personal and organizational factors as intertwined, I have arbitrarily presented the personal issues first. Following that are the organizational factors the teachers selected and which I arranged according to the time and importance the participants appeared to place on them during the interviews.

Personal Factors

Although the lives of the six participants in this study appear relatively stable at the moment, such was not always the case. Two had to deal with divorce at a young age and during the process, one lost her most valued support, the backing of her parents. Five have dealt with the death of a parent, close friend, or spouse. Support from their family was very important in enabling these teachers to keep going following traumas, but it seems to have been heavily buttressed with support from school.

> See, I can remember when my mother was dying of cancer and I'm getting phone calls, "Your mom's going into the hospital." My principal was so wonderful to me. I mean, there was no question. He said, "You get in that car and you go." He was there through it all with me. He was there at my mother's funeral. He was there at my father's. He really kept me on a even keel 'cause he was very concerned and very supportive. I really would not have survived that whole situation without that kind of support, knowing that I could go if I needed to go. (Mary)

> Cindy [a colleague and mentor] came to the hospital and held my hand. If I hadn't had that job and beginning to come full circle in feeling really confident in myself, I'm not sure if I'd have continued on. Cindy made me feel so confident. (Amy)

> I was going to work on report cards the day I got the call that she had passed away. I spend so much time on report cards — my mind just was not clear — I couldn't deal with it. So I wrote a note to the parents explaining that there had been a death in my family, that report cards are important to me, but that they'd be late. But I think if I had to deal with the stress that I dealt with that week for a long time — I don't know [pause]. Maybe I'd have to take a leave of absence because that wouldn't be fair to the children [in the class]. It's *very* scary. That was very hard for me. But one thing I will say, the teachers in my school were extremely supportive and the parents were very supportive. I had cards sent to me from my students' parents and people would come up to me and say how sorry they were. I mean, the outpouring of caring was just unbelievable. (Camille)

All of the teachers talked about the many varied levels of collegial friendships that they have appreciated over their career. Additionally, they enjoy different kinds of support from their family or spouse: from household chores to listening; from helping to decorate the classroom to an appreciation of the difficulties of teaching. Several of the participants, from closely observing their own children grow and develop, have a particular understanding or awareness of their students' development or problems.

Organization of personal matters also appears to play a role in juggling teaching and renewal. Five of the participants were able to devote large amounts of time and energy to the first six or seven years of their teaching career either because they were single or because they did not have children until later. Today, Elizabeth and Donna have never had children, Mary and Amy have children who are now adult, and Camille and Irene have adolescent children at home. For the latter, unless there is a family emergency, school still comes first, even though it sometimes means making difficult decisions.

> I can't say, if there was a family emergency, you know, that teaching would come before my family. My family would come first. But when things are ticking, teaching comes first. And we had an instance today [sigh]. My son had an important appointment today at 5:00 — my husband, my son, and I. At 3:30, I had a parent conference, and the parent came late, a little after 4:00. And so, I had a choice to make — and I met with the parent and called my husband and missed the appointment. Bill [her husband] said, "How could you do that? This is your son. Why didn't you just tell the parent you couldn't?" But this was a real important conference and I had to make a decision there. I mean, if there would not have been a husband, if I were a single parent, I would have had no choice. But I knew Bill was there and I knew he could handle it.

The same kind of tension, produced by wanting to do her best as a teacher and as a parent, seems evident in Irene's stories, although she admits that her ethnic and religious upbringing have probably influenced her image of a mother's role as one of selfless support. She cannot imagine, for herself or for other women, making any choices that would appear to be putting one's self before one's children. She talked about the tension she feels when school and family duties clash.

> Every year, I do a kindergarten orientation where the parents come with the child. Yet when my children had orientation, I couldn't go because I was teaching kindergarten. My children's first day of school, I couldn't be there to put them on the bus because I had to be at *my* school with fifty other kids. It's hard because the parent in me wants to be with [my kids], but the teacher's saying, "I can't be." I overheard a teacher talking about how she took the day off to spend with Jamie [her son] and his class. I had mixed feelings because part of me is thinking, "Oh that's so neat that she took the day off to be with Jamie and his class," but then I'm thinking, "That really wasn't right to her class. She's being mommy, but yet . . ."

Irene has made specific career choices around her family. She recognized a personal desire to work after the birth of her children and compromised by working half time for a number of years so that she could be a parent volunteer in her children's

school. She has largely abandoned the idea of going back to university for a doctoral degree although it was something she personally wanted to do.

> I read about people — people who are working on their Master's [degree] —
> and I think, "Oh, I'm so glad I did all that before I had kids." The thought of
> me pursuing a Ph.D. [degree] with children is not *me* because — and my
> husband says, "I'll divorce you. There is no way." He knows *me* and there's
> Irene as a mother and Irene as a teacher. I would love to do it, but would
> never do it because I would jeopardize my marriage and my kids. Because I
> don't see them as much as I want to see them, now that I'm working full
> time. Stuff for myself will be some day — later. What I can do now, I can
> kind of balance. I can get most of it done at school. I'm there at seven in the
> morning. I can take home what I need to take home. There's never enough
> time. You could spend infinity at school, but yet I have it down to a science
> to the extent that's capable and I can still go home and get my children to
> where they need to go.

Balance for the teachers was linked to the amount of stability and change in
their lives at any given time (what Gardner, 1963/1981, referred to as a balanced
framework or system for renewal). As Amy explained, "I like new things, not on a
constant basis, but enough at the right time." Three teachers commented that after a
trauma, particularly if other changes were happening simultaneously, their patterns
of renewal were interrupted or stopped. Mary halted her art work for a time; Amy
put off all renewal for awhile, having recognized that she had depleted her energy;
Elizabeth continued with house renovations and a graduate course, but was sick a
lot that year. Over time, they have learned that balance or a change of pace or
activity is necessary to their well-being and to their teaching.

> When I couldn't exercise, I started not handling stress as well. I wasn't as
> tolerant [in the classroom]. I put a lot into my job, but if I had to choose, it
> doesn't come first. Relationships come first, definitely. When I go home, I
> need to focus on my family. And I think because of that, I can give to my
> job. I can't live education 24 hours a day. I have to learn how to shut it off
> and it makes me a better teacher in the long run. Somehow it goes hand in
> hand. (Amy)

> I'll just get so bogged down on onelittle thing or one little problem or "I've
> got to get this done! I've got to get this done!" It's nice to step away from
> that situation and realize you are a person. There *is* life beyond that class-
> room! [laugh] And it's fun. It's fun to teach, but it's also fun to do some-

thing very different, something where you're not pushing and you're not in charge. I pity the teachers who never attempt to try anything new — don't have any professional journals, don't look at any new magazines, never go in a children's bookstore and sit there. I've learned. It's been a long time coming, but I have learned that I need to take time. Everybody does. You cannot keep up with everything. (Elizabeth)

Professionalism

Of the selected contextual factors (professionalism, colleagues, resources, and district support) that enable and/or constrain renewal, the teachers put great emphasis on professionalism. During the interviews, whether discussing their personal or professional life, they invariably talked about professionalism and respect as necessary and vital conditions for allowing them to do their best. This corroborated the literature indicating that mutual respect may be an essential ingredient in most authentic forms of teaching and learning (Willie and Howey, 1980) and that teachers are stimulated by respect from relevant adults (Joyce and Showers, 1988; Louis, 1992; Louis and Smith, 1990; McLaughlin and Yee, 1988). For Mary, professionalism includes being informed, being treated as a responsible adult, and practicing diplomacy in all social interactions.

I think maybe one of the things would be that you would look at things more globally: Instead of seeing the trees, you would see the whole forest. You have to understand the system and where you're coming from. You have to know that there are limits to what you *can* do according to what system you're in. You have to be able to adjust yourself to every new principal that comes in, and how *they* treat you sometimes affects how you feel as a professional — whether they are treating you like one of the children [laugh] or with lesson plans, if they just leave you alone and say, "I expect you to have them." You have to develop a working attitude with them because a lot of the things that you want to try, if you don't have that rapport with that principal, they won't allow you to do it. I think you have to act professionally with the parents. You have to be able to present yourself, both in speech and in manner, in a way that people know that you are open to them but that you are also the professional there. So you really have to be diplomatic, very diplomatic in your dealings with everybody: your parents, the children, other staff members. Mutual respect.

Other ingredients of professionalism included dependability (being punctual and being prepared), cooperation, fairness, willingness to ask for and share information and ideas, freedom to give opinions, feeling successful or proud of one's work, and working hard for children ("trying to find ways to make things better in the classroom, better for the children and better for themselves"). However, the underlying themes invariably included human relations and continuous learning.

> Well, I think one who is in a field where they're dealing with the public, be it teachers or parents or children, needs to maintain a certain level of professionalism and that means to deal honestly and openly with people, to be a diligent worker and do the very best that you can at whatever it is that you're doing, and to respect your colleagues and continually keep up with your own personal education. I don't think one's learning ever stops. I think that it is a duty of our profession, in education, to keep ourselves abreast of what's going on currently. I don't think training from 20 years ago is the same as training now; that's why going back and taking courses and becoming involved in inservices is crucial to knowing what's going on today. (Camille)

Collegiality

Several different kinds of collegiality with adults emerged from the data and within each, there were also varying depths of relationships. Recognizable divisions of collegiality included:

1. teacher/teacher;
2. teacher/principal;
3. teacher/parents of students;
4. teacher/mentor;
5. teacher/teacher educator (e.g., resource leader, professor).

The most important relationships for the participants were with their peers, not necessarily at the same school. For example, Amy has been on summer curriculum writing teams and explained that she is closer to those teachers than the people she works with during the year. Sources for finding colleagues included sororities, graduate school, curriculum writing teams, teachers' sports teams, reading recovery training, team planning sessions, resource roles, and professional development meetings. Whatever the source, the teachers learned to know the philosophy, work ethic, and strengths of each other. This information, and the willingness of the colleague to share and be open to new ideas, seems to build the foundation for close collegiality.

Not only do the participants see their close colleagues as supportive, they value them as sources of ideas and information. They think nothing of calling a colleague to say, "Hey, I was going to try this. You've done it. Do you think this will work?" Or sometimes:

It's nice to know what's happening in other schools. Then you get ideas for yourself, but you also feel, "Oh, everybody's doing it" or "They're all having a problem this year." Or you get the gossip, "Glenbrook school is going to try this new idea." "This school's piloting a new math program, so next year they'll probably be hitting us with it." And then we can call up and find out, "Do you know that book?" or "Do you have whatever?" You can borrow things which is great. I enjoy that. (Elizabeth)

Invariably, the teachers did not separate their personal and professional lives in their close collegial relationships, although the professional relationship seemed to come first. Sometimes collegial relationships were extended to close personal friendships that involved out-of-school socializing as well, although this was usually mentioned in connection with team partners; in other words, teachers with whom they had spent a great deal of time. Many of these deep friendships have survived over distance and time. In one case, having that kind of friendship allowed two teachers to function in a school climate they found unprofessional and largely unsupportive of their work and teaching style.

Balancing an imbalance of power
As noted earlier, mutual respect is crucial to these teachers' sense of professionalism. Age and years of teaching experience do not appear to be barriers to teacher/teacher collegiality.

People ask me questions all the time. They feel I've had a variety of experiences. New teachers, teachers my age, people with equal experience will sit down and want to discuss various ways of doing things and plan things. And I feel really good that my peers come to me for that kind of thing and that I can equally go to them. So that's a feeling of professionalism when your opinion is asked for and valued. You're asked to give inservices to your own staff. I think if I didn't feel respected [long pause] — I don't figure that people are going to come to me and ask me questions if I'm coming off pompous. I want to be successful without having to be one of those people who walks around holier-than-thou. I just can't stand that and I think I go out of my way just being "real," and to me, that's a true professional too. (Amy)

Rosenholtz (1989) noted that "hierarchical control and professionalism, like sibling rivals, do not get along well with each other" although that is not to say that one is all bad or all good (p. 215). Berman (1987) also inferred a relationship between power and professionalism, while Gardner (1963/1981) emphasized the necessity of a tradition of vigorous criticism (p. xvii) and freedom of thought in order for renewal to flourish (p. 33). Those themes were underscored by the participants, especially issues of power in teacher/principal or teacher/mentor relationship. They appear to be impressed not by a title or position, but by the knowledge, performance, openness to others' concerns or reasoning, and integrity of "superiors."

> I feel I'll do a good job no matter who the principal is, whether I like him or not. But I feel that I'll try even harder if I respect that person and think that they're working hard too for the children. Even if they don't agree with me! A couple times, I didn't agree with my principal, but I still respect him because I know he sees what's going on and he's always willing to let you have a chance to explain to him. It was the same thing with Francis. I respected him because if you could defend yourself and you could make points about *why* you believed something or *why* you felt it was going to be better, he would let you explain. Then he would make a decision — and it still may not go your way, but he always let you explain. He never made a judgment *without* giving you his reason for it and letting you give your reason for it. (Elizabeth)

All of the participants have had at least one valued collegial teacher/principal or teacher/mentor relationship. In each case, the superior seems to have worked at diminishing any perceptions of unequal roles. Amy's administrator appears to take seriously the original definition of "administer" meaning to "minister to" or to "serve" (Huebner, 1987, p. 27). This has enabled Amy's renewal and won her deep respect.

> I'm working for an administrator right now who is just a master at that. He does *his* job and helps us with ours. There's the difference. And when they had the first "Bosses' Day," the man turned twenty-two thousand shades of red and said, "I hate that word. My role is not to be a boss; it's to be here to help you all." And he lives it every day of his life. Have you seen these very quiet but very effective people? He's one of those — very laid back, but very effective. Child-oriented and staff-oriented. I can talk to him as an equal. He doesn't play these *games*. We go in and we talk about the system, we talk about things, we can be very frank, we can be — I can just *talk* to him. I don't have to worry about playing any word games. He is a very real, honest, upright person. He is exactly what he says he is. He lives it. He's got the good of *all* at heart. His teachers will follow him to the end of the earth — and have, from building to building.

While the teachers have worked for principals who have supported their teaching and who appreciated their efforts to self-renew, only Amy has had the kind of relationship that pushed her professional renewal and desire for renewal to new heights.

> I only had that job with Cindy [her supervisor and mentor] for a very short time, but I can't tell you how much I learned. It was my "doctorate" [laugh]. That's how I figure it. It was wonderful! It was then that I really read Lucy Calkins and Donald Graves and got into the whole philosophy of the thing, and learned to put all these wonderful words with what I had been doing, but I didn't have all the right labels for. It was great! I loved it! Cindy made me feel so confident. I could get out and tackle the whole school system — stand up for what I believe. She believed in me: told me guidelines of what I was to accomplish and headed me in the right direction and pretty much trusted me. It was a trust she had in me to go out and inservice and say the right things, and come back and check with her and talk with her. I could tell philosophically we were really on the same track. We identified as people and women, as well as professionally. She said, "Hey, there's a conference coming up. I think you should present." So I presented at major conferences, and did things like that. It was wonderful!

Leadership and teacher renewal

In schools with a collaborative culture, almost all claimed to have teacher leaders who are receptive to trying new ideas, capable of inspiring others, and willing to share in solving individual or school problems (Rosenholtz, 1989, p. 64-66). That the teachers in this study have not regularly had this kind of support and encouragement indicates that their renewal has surely not been enthusiastically supported to the degree it could have been, given such responsive learners. As the following poignant comment indicates, teachers can only imagine or occasionally glimpse how administrators' control or lack of knowing how to encourage them has affected their learning.

> I think a principal encouraging people to stretch their wings, to fly a little bit higher than they did before, really makes a difference. I don't think I've ever had one who really wanted you to stretch your wings. I think sometimes they might have been afraid of what might happen if you would. (Mary)

If, by the teachers' definition, professionalism includes learning, then teachers need opportunities to "stretch their wings" and at least some colleagues with the knowledge and ability to enable them to find those opportunities. Only occasionally did the teachers in this study find those qualities in colleagues in a position of power.

Collegial networks and career development

Because all six teachers have participated in various professional activities at the district level, they have met many colleagues. Four appear to have a very extensive range of colleagues. One kind of collegial relationship acts as a political network. It is a network that enables renewal, particularly career development, by facilitating new opportunities, positions, or roles.

The network includes current and former principals, teachers, administrative supervisors (of term appointed resource personnel), Peer Assistance and Review (PAR) teachers, mentors, teacher aides, educators in the state Department of Education, district coordinators, professors, reading recovery leaders, and special projects leaders. These are the people who have called to ask the participants to take part in curriculum projects, to attend or present at conferences, to take student teachers, to pilot programs, to design and present workshops to peers, to read proposals, to accept community visitors and teacher interns in their classrooms, to try out sample books from publishers, and the like.

This network has also been highly instrumental in facilitating school transfers or finding new positions for the teachers, as well as writing letters of recommendation for them. When Elizabeth completed a term appointment as a resource leader and wanted to return to the classroom, she got a phone call that a position was opening in a school whose principal she had known earlier as a supervisor in the district office building.

> The teacher aide at Gord's school was a friend of mine 'cause I'd known her from before. She called me up and said, "One of our first grade teachers is retiring. I'll tell Gord you want the job and he'll call down for you, but you've got to fill out the paper today." So I called Mrs. Bodon [a principal who had once interviewed Elizabeth, but who now works at district headquarters]. "Well now," she said, "I've been shifted to a different department, but I'll call [a colleague] and she's a friend of Gord."

Camille attended her first national reading conference thanks to her network.

> It was the first national conference I ever attended and it was very exciting because not only did I go as a participant, but I was a presenter as well. The professor called me. I have a personal relationship with her, as well as a professional relationship. She called me and asked me if I wanted to be a part of this panel.

Later, she was invited to attend a national math conference because the coordinator for whom she had earlier piloted a math program had received a Grant that covered the cost of the substitute teacher.

Almost all of the contacts within the teachers' networks led to further career development or a new position or assignment. Once the network started, it constantly expanded as the teachers met still more colleagues. The excitement and stimulation that the new contacts and renewal generated seem to override the politics involved, although one teacher commented that you have to know "the game." In turn, several of the teachers have now begun to assist their peers in a similar way such as mentoring young teachers and suggesting colleagues' names as writing team members or workshop presenters.

Transfers: A Search for Enabling Renewal

When Hoy, Tarter, and Kottkamp (1991) proffered their questionnaire as a useful heuristic for understanding practices that support open and healthy school climates, they honed in on collegiality: The questionnaire examines the interactions between teacher/principal and teacher/teacher. Supportive behavior by the principal includes openness to teacher suggestions, respect for the professional competence of the teacher, and a personal and professional interest in each teacher. This behavior is in contrast to rigid monitoring (directive behavior) and demands that interfere with teaching (restrictive behavior).

Collegial behavior among teachers is described as supportive of open, professional interaction and respectful of colleagues' competence. Intimate behavior goes further and includes personal and/or social relationships. Disengaged behavior is reflected in a lack of support, group effort, or professional cohesion or respect.

The results of the questionnaire by the participants in this study (Appendix D) coupled with the interview data indicate that positive social interactions are extremely important to the participants and that these teachers deliberately transfer from schools that they perceived to be "closed and unhealthy" to schools that had a reputation for being "open and healthy." It appears as though teacher/teacher relationships have a greater influence on transfers than the principal/teacher relationship, although both play a role in the decision to transfer.

There also seems to be a critical mass of teacher support necessary for survival in an unhealthy school, as well as a critical mass of teacher support necessary to maintain a climate of open teacher behavior in the face of a directive or restrictive principal. While various teachers referred to this critical mass, its nature remains obscure. However, there is no doubt that when teachers are in open, healthy schools (see Appendix D for the perceptions of Amy, Camille, and Mary), they value and appreciate what they have. Once they have worked in such a climate but find themselves in schools with disengaged staffs and/or directive principals (see Appendix D for the perceptions of Donna and Elizabeth), they start to think about transferring.

Principal/teacher dimensions

Earlier, Mary described the personal support she was given by her principal and said she did not know whether she could have recovered from the death of her parents without the principal's strong personal and professional support. That principal was at the school for over a decade and became part of a very cohesive staff interested in continuous improvement.

> You're with them every day. I mean, they're like family. And sure, we have squabbles and stuff going on, but the underlying thing is that we care about each other. And we mostly care about the students. It's especially interesting when you get new people into the building. They can't believe how friendly we are, how open the staff is toward change. If you show us a better way of doing things, we'll be right there pushing behind you. I think it's a mix of things. I think it's the mix of people. I think, too, that it had to do with having the open center and you had to work with each other. I think also having [a stable staff] — I think we evolved as a staff. You can even deal around a non-supportive principal if the rest of the teachers are with you. You find ways.

When a new principal arrived and did not contribute to the health of the school, the staff closed ranks and were instrumental in his hasty departure. Teachers do not stay in this school so they can fall into a comfortable routine, but because it is a place that enables them to renew and do their best teaching.

Although another veteran teacher knew of cases where teachers had united against a principal, the teachers recognize that principals "can make or break a building." What these veteran teachers also realize, however, is that they have the option to transfer and that change can be healthy.

> You can feel atmosphere when you walk into a building and most of the time, it is principal oriented. They can make or break a school: They are the building block; they are the foundation. You can walk in — I mean, there are some schools where there is just everything so regimented. I mean, there is just no flexibility to anything. The demands are just unreal and irrational. I absolutely could not work for a principal like that at this stage of the game. It would really be difficult. I would, one way or the other, escape a school like that at this point in my career. Those of us that have been around in a variety of schools tend to do that. (Amy)

Donna considers herself fortunate to have been assigned to what she perceived as a healthy school for her first teaching position. Not only did she have a personal and professional relationship with her principal, her socialization to teaching included a structured summer staff retreat, informal "happy hours" after school on Fridays, taking graduate courses with colleagues, and socializing with colleagues on weekends. When her first principal left, a number of teachers left too, leaving new teachers who are perceived to be disengaged from the philosophy and goals the original staff values. Already disenchanted, Donna found the new principal to be the deciding factor in her decision to transfer (see Appendix D).

Yes, definitely he's a source [of my wanting to leave] even though security-wise, it's a lot easier to stay there. I know every student in the building, I know all the teachers, I know the principal, parents. It makes it very easy, but if I really want to broaden my experience, I need to move on. I need to push myself for my own personal [sake], you know. I think the change would be good for me. I don't want to get into a routine. I don't want to waste myself and I want to be somewhere where I really feel I can make a difference. So I'm searching. That's part of going to these inservices and talking with teachers and making mental notes of buildings that you hear are working and buildings that you hear that aren't working. It really makes a difference.

The perception of wasting one's potential by not being allowed to do one's best teaching was a theme that was described in several different ways.

Oh, she [the principal] was a gem! I had this lovely room where I could have had a center and I wanted to put in a typewriter for the kids. I wanted to have a tape recorder and she would not allow me to have a plug in my room. [laugh] She had all the sinks pulled out of the rooms because she said they cause trouble. It was very depressing. I felt awful. Here I was, given the opportunity to buy some materials and things, and I had a room where I could have those kids working and talking and acting 'cause I wanted to do some role play and do drama and all kinds of creative work with books — and was not allowed to! Oh! I hated that year! I just hated it! (Elizabeth)

There was no flexibility [in the new position]. Which meant I was working at this building doing something that philosophically was against my better judgment. And only to a certain degree was I successful, and I was miserable and they were miserable. So I decided after one year, I left it. I could *not* — I mean, there wasn't enough play in it. I was only allowed to see the kids for 40 minutes at a time, and I'm not a 40 minute person, not even close. So it was against *everything* in me: I didn't agree with the focus of the job; I didn't agree with any of it — just *any* of it. And I wasn't even doing the school that much good. I felt totally wasted. I hated it. (Amy)

Teacher/teacher dimensions

Even when teachers feel good about their teaching, they may transfer because their closest colleagues are leaving the school. Irene and Elizabeth had the experience of being part of a team whose members, for various reasons, had to transfer. Rather than stay in the school as part of a new team, they opted to leave at the same time. Said Irene, "The opportunity is now and it will never be the same, so I'm going to go." Amy and Camille mentioned that they too have either transferred from a school at the same time as a colleague or, like Elizabeth, have applied to schools in which they had friends.

In one school, Amy enjoyed her work and her colleagues, but not the principal: "I could get so involved with the team that I could ignore her [the principal] or work around her. After my resource job [a short appointment at the district level], she pretty much left me alone." But Amy eventually felt held back by her team and, compelled by an urge to improve her teaching and innovate, chose to transfer rather than coerce the team into what she wanted to do.

I really got to the point where I wanted to try things that the team couldn't buy into and I needed to move off on my own. I felt constrained and I felt I was doing things [that] philosophically I had already moved away from. But to not do it would have been like not cooperating with the team and I didn't want to be in that position. It was time [to leave].

Camille talked about the agony she felt in making a transfer decision that would separate her from her team partner. They had met earlier, become friends, and had applied for a team position. Unhappy with the negative and unprofessional attitude in the school even though they loved their program, they were in the dilemma of Camille having an opportunity to transfer to a well regarded school and her team mate possibly having to stay behind alone.

I interviewed and was offered that job. So then I had a very tough decision to make: Do I go or do I stay? It was very, very difficult. I had loyalty to — well, Marg was not sure she was going to stay either. If she was going to stay, there would not have been a choice for me; I would have stayed too. But she told me she was not sure she was staying, that she was going to look at other options, and that I should take the job. So, I debated and debated and I called all kinds of people and asked for advice, and finally I just decided that, with Marg's blessing, I was going to [transfer]. We worked that out.

The reasons given by these teachers for transferring include the need to renew themselves, the belief that they are not able to do their best job teaching in a given school, the belief that their services are not being utilized, an overly directive and restrictive principal, a job that runs counter to their philosophy, one or more colleagues also leaving the school, and a school climate they perceive to be unhealthy and distracting. It appears as though there is a fine line between what counts as adequate support and what cannot sustain their efforts.

If the principal interfered with the teaching, then there's no doubt, that would be the more important thing. I'd have to leave. 'Cause you can have a lot of supplies and things, but if you're not allowed to work with the children in a way that makes you feel like you're really truly doing something, then no, that's not teaching. Like I said though, if you get a support group — and I've seen that in buildings where they were united against the principal — and it worked fine, as long as nobody left. But if you have no one else who understands what you're going through and is supportive of that, then I would leave. If I had no other teacher support, I *would* leave. (Elizabeth)

We were placed in a building that had very few people the way we are. So that made us very uncomfortable. We had people say to us, you know, "Why are you hanging up your children's work? You're making us look bad." We had people say that to us! And we just — displaying work was the way we did things. It was all-the-way and it was creative and it was so children could get something positive. It was like a collision of attitudes because there were a lot of people in that building who felt that those children can't possibly learn. It wasn't everyone; it was *some* people there. So being in an environment like that was very difficult to work in, especially when we were working so hard and going to graduate school. We needed support. There were several teachers there who were wonderful: There was a small group of Primary teachers in that building who were supportive and who encouraged us and were great. But on the *whole*, it was very difficult to work there. We had each other, but it was a very stifling situation because you couldn't do what you wanted to do and have it received well. They were always looking for something negative. There was just like an underlying current there. In some buildings, maybe there's one or two negative people, and you know, you can just kind of tune them out or whatever, but there were too many negatives in this particular building. We both said we each had another life [laugh] and this was not worth it. (Camille)

Resources and District Support

Resources as a factor that can enable or constrain renewal was given short shrift by the participants although several pointed out that resources were much more important to them at the beginning of their career. Now, however, they joke about their boxes of resources filling the basement or garage. As Irene explained, "I have a wealth [of resources] which I have purchased or made. Materials don't make the teacher, but they certainly help." Amy has "thousands of dollars worth of books" she has purchased. Camille and Elizabeth have a passion for cruising bookstores, "only the problem is, you don't just look, you buy." Mary and Donna also invest in books for children.

What is immediately recognizable in listening to these teachers is that they see everything and everybody as possible resources. They get ideas and/or materials from colleagues, parents, students, conferences, workshops, the central warehouse for the district, community personnel and stores or agencies, spouses, district resource leaders, the public library, the Chamber of Commerce — and on and on. Amy noted that the one resource she really appreciates is a well-equipped school library with multiple copies of books, but that she can still do a good job with her own resources and contacts.

As for district support, although it was duly noted that there is more now than fifteen or twenty years ago, these teachers seem to continue their renewal with or without district support. For example, twenty years ago, Camille and Elizabeth were each part of self-initiated small groups of teachers who met at each other's houses on weekends to create materials and share ideas. More recently, when little support accompanied the shift from basal readers to whole language, several of the teachers found help on their own from colleagues, books, and the university. The teachers agreed that there is now much more emphasis on staff development. There is also a 45 minute early dismissal for the children once a month so teachers can engage in staff development. Its value appears to depend on the creativity of the principal.

There was high praise for the opportunity to participate on writing teams in the summer since this career development was seen as stimulating and as a means of influencing the direction of education. The district pays an hourly wage for that work, as well as for the inservice presentations the teachers give for implementation in various schools. There was also excitement that the district is attempting to offer an alternative to inservice training. For example, Donna and Elizabeth, who have taken reading recovery training on their own, do not have to attend the reading workshops and may choose a conference instead. But for the most part, the teachers perceive the district workshops to be repetitious, pulling teachers out of their classroom but offering them little. Both Donna and Elizabeth commented that they are at the point where they consider a workshop valuable if they get one new idea.

However, the major problems these teachers face come from the district directly and indirectly. The direct problem is a lack of substitute teachers to cover classes of teachers who are presenting or attending workshops. Workshops then are canceled or postponed. The indirect pressure is that the teachers feel terribly guilty if they leave their class, even though they would love release time to attend conferences or visit other schools or districts. Even as a resource teacher, Amy felt "like [she] was playing hooky just being in a car during the day." Elizabeth said, "Last year, I did attend the reading recovery conference for one day so I didn't have to take a day off school. I attended the Sunday session." Others also attend what they can after school, on weekends, and during the summer because of the hassle and guilt associated with absence from the classroom.

> The way our school situation is, it's like if you take a day off, you feel like you're penalizing the children and being penalized yourself. Now the state's looking at how many days teachers are gone because that's harmful to children. So therefore, if I go for a week [for a conference or mini sabbatical], I must really be messing up the kids. Another thing, it's very hard to get a sub. A lot of times you're not there and there's no sub at all. Then your kids are spread around, so then you're worried the other teachers are mad at you. So here you are: You can't go for this training because, God forbid, the subs go for sick people more than for people at workshops. That's also a constraint in the classroom. If people are stressed out and upset and need a day off, they feel like, "I better not take that day 'cause I'll mess up my kids." There you are; you just get sicker. I tend to do that. You figure, "I'll wait. I'll be fine. All I have to do is get through to the weekend." Then you spend the weekend in bed. You go through the year that way. That is hard. And I know we do have a professional leave fund, but we're constantly being told, "Only this many people can go and if you went last year, you can't go next year and you can only spend this much money. You spent all that money, so you took up somebody else's time and money." And then, you have a hard time finding out — it's like at the last minute, they'll say they approved it. By then, it's too late to apply. (Elizabeth)

Camille, as well as several of the other participants, has spent a lot of personal time in search of renewal. It is renewal that is never factored into the understanding of what it is to be a teacher; nor is it recognized by the district.

We get very few professional days to go around, but through my graduate work, I did have the opportunity to visit classrooms through classes that I took and they worked it out. And I spend some days — when my spring break or my days off are different than the suburban districts, I've gone around to other classrooms. Like before I got into reading recovery, I went and observed reading recovery 'cause I had heard about it and I was curious. The workshop style of teaching — I had not seen that in action, so I went to a suburban school to observe that because I was curious. You know, you hear about things through friends and colleagues and it's real nice to go and watch it, so I do that whenever possible but I'm not afforded with the luxury of taking off. Certainly in my own building, we do go around when we can to see what's going on in other classrooms and that's also very worthwhile. But even looking at what someone else has on a bulletin board is very stimulating.

It was evident in listening to these exemplary teachers that their professional renewal has been sought at great personal cost, both in time and money.

Dealing with Constraints

As mentioned above, teachers use transfers as a way to deal with the constraint of a school climate they perceive to be closed and unhealthy. Their breadth of interest and involvement and finding a balance that works also help minimize difficulties in one area of the teachers' personal or professional lives. For example, when Amy was dealing with a personal trauma, "work became [her] stability." Donna noted that knowledge of the system helped keep her work in the classroom in perspective. These teachers have found a balance between spending time with children and time with adults. Thus their collegial network is very important to them. Over time, they have realized that "you can't live school twenty-four hours a day," but their personal renewal is nevertheless intertwined with their professional performance; it allows them to face their work refreshed.

Five of the teachers have dealt with the district constraint of getting very little release time for attending conferences, institutes, courses, and workshops by participating after school, on weekends, and during vacations. Five participants in particular deal with this constraint by giving enormous amounts of personal time to their renewal which, for the most part, is unrecognized and uncompensated despite the benefits to the district. Irene has chosen to limit this kind of renewal more than the other participants so that she can spend time with her children. Even so, by spending ten-hour days at school, she manages to fit in considerable renewal. Also at school, the teachers have students and parent volunteers help them as much as possible, thus freeing up time for professional involvement and collegial conversations. Many evenings, weekends, and summers are spent making or seeking resources or engaging in personal and professional renewal.

Several of the teachers have deliberately volunteered to join writing teams and to sit on district committees in an attempt to influence what happens in classrooms. One joined the district's Promotion/Retention Committee in order to influence assessment practices while others have spent summers examining alternative methods of assessment. They will stand up for their principles, but have learned to prioritize to retain energy for teaching: "You've got to choose your battle. So I pick the ones that are the most important to my survival and to the kids' survival and those are the ones I go after." Five of the participants have learned to understand and use the political system in the district to try "to make a difference" and they willingly give personal time to do so.

Discussion

What emerged from the participants' stories led me to conclude that the personal and professional worlds in which these teachers live are so complex that factors may be both enabling and constraining depending on the context, people, or time involved. For example, family members may be supportive, as in the case of Mary's lawsuit, but may be the source of guilt when choices have to be made between time for family and time for personal or professional renewal, particularly for Irene. Resources seemed to be quite a priority at the beginning of these teachers' careers; less so as they built up their own collections, networks, and knowledge of sources. Two factors in particular emerged as very important, both having potential to enable or constrain the participants' ability to do their best work. The two factors are teacher/teacher collegiality and the teacher/principal relationship, together influencing school climate.

The factor that appeared to enable renewal the most consistently was supportive colleagues. (It should be noted, however, that when teachers were unhappy in schools, it was most often because they perceived that too many of their colleagues were unsupportive. "Unsupportive" includes teachers who are perceived as not excited about learning or teaching, not caring about students, and not carrying their share of work at school.) The critical mass that determines "too many" unsupportive colleagues is unknown. The participants do not necessarily work in the same school as their closest colleagues; they may stay in touch through telephone conversations, working on projects or writing teams together, and socializing. However, they do enjoy working with other high-performing teachers (also see Campbell, 1988).

The level of involvement in renewal activities is directly related to the breadth of their collegial network. For example, Irene limits her involvement to exclude evenings, weekends, and summers as much as possible. On the other hand, because she has worked in so many schools over nearly two decades, she nonetheless has an extensive network. All of the participants see their colleagues as resources for helping them improve their teaching and learning. They enjoy giving and receiving pedagogical ideas and resources, finding out what is happening in the district, exchanging opinions, seeking advice, getting support, discussing professional issues, and occasionally, socializing.

Within the broad context of colleagues as an enabling factor is a collegial network that is more political. This group of colleagues has been particularly helpful to the participants in their career development by facilitating new opportunities, positions, or roles for them. The participants have drawn on this network to transfer from one school to another or to get letters of recommendation. Often, their colleagues are in a position to suggest conferences, to issue invitations to participate on writing teams, to nominate teachers to pilot projects or present workshops, and the like. These veteran participants are now in a position where they are starting to do the same for some of their colleagues.

Each participant has had at least one principal they have admired and respected. Their comments indicate that these teachers appreciate being treated as equal adults, having the opportunity to express their opinions, and hearing justification for the principal's decisions. They want to see evidence of the principal's interest in children and learning, they expect fairness, and they enjoy straightforward communication and depth of instructional knowledge. Integrity of character, an ethic of care, consistency between actions and words, and openness to innovation were important to them in describing their perceptions of principals they respect.

A major constraint by principals is interference with teaching. These teachers continue to go to great lengths to improve their teaching and while they hope the principal supports their efforts, they have learned to ignore or "work around" those who are neutral or those who do not make their job easier. Task autonomy is so important to one teacher that she said she would transfer if the principal interfered with classroom teaching. There was unanimous agreement among the veteran teachers that principals who have been out of the classroom for several years carry little credibility when it comes to daily classroom practice. The teachers seem to be at a point in their careers where opportunities to learn (for their students and themselves) can best be supported with organizational assistance and flexibility that allows them to reach their goals.

Rosenholtz (1989) suggested that attitudes at the top echelons of district administration filter down through the administrators and teachers to create moving systems (self-renewing) or stuck systems (non-renewing). The data in this study indicate that the interplay of various pieces of the puzzle may be very changeable over time and that renewal of these teachers may be hindered, but is unlikely to be stopped, by school climate, administrators, or superintendents.

Apart from involuntary transfers (resulting from low seniority, school closures, and so forth), transfers or lack of transfers by the teachers in this study were quite deliberate. Goodlad (1983) observed that the more satisfying schools were those that self-renewed; that is, that undertook continuous evaluation of programs, examined alternative procedures, and had faculty willing to try new ideas (pp. 54-55). When the teachers in this study found such a school, as Mary did many years ago, they tended to stay there as long as self-renewal could occur. Mary has chosen to transfer to different grade levels as a source of self-renewal, but has stayed in this school many years, appreciating an environment in which she feels she can do her best and recognizing colleagues who support learning and who have built intimate collegial relationships. These kinds of schools seem to encourage respect for individuals and treating others as equals, both very important ingredients of professionalism for these teachers.

While the teachers seem to agree that "a principal can make or break a school," they quietly "find ways" to create a workable climate for themselves and locate supportive colleagues, or else they leave the school. Each teacher works hard to get along with colleagues, contribute to the school, and to find or create support within the school. However, when their teaching is not supported by the administrator, when the administrator's beliefs about teaching/learning are opposed to their own, or the administrator interferes with their classroom teaching, the teachers look for a school whose climate will support their beliefs and style of teaching.

The same holds true for colleagues, although the critical mass of support is unknown. What is known, however, is that collegial support is so important to these teachers that when team mates left a given school, their choice influenced the participant's decision to transfer as well. Similarly, it was noted that teachers will transfer to find or stay with a highly effective principal.

The importance of professionalism in the lives of these teachers was an unanticipated finding of the study. It appears as though the foundation of their clear vision of professionalism may have been formed early in their career as they team taught with others. Their definition of professionalism invariably included continuous learning and skilled social interactions. It may be that in describing a professional, they were also defining an exemplary teacher.

An Ethic of Care

For let no one be deceived, the important things that happen in the schools result from the interaction of personalities. Children and teachers are not disembodied intelligences, not instructing machines and learning machines, but whole human beings tied together in a complex maze of social interconnections.

Waller (1965, p. 1)

Care and commitment, along with continuous learning, are major characteristics attributed to exemplary teachers in the literature. While care and commitment were not investigated as part of the research questions and therefore did not appear in the interview schedules, the participants referred to them directly or indirectly in the course of conversation.

As noted earlier, when the participants recalled wonderful teachers they had had as children, the words "caring," "nurturing," and "compassionate" were used to describe them. Camille remembers "a unique teacher" she had in first grade. The teacher had told her class she was going to Spain for vacation and had taught Spanish at recess to interested students. That summer, each of her students received a postcard from Spain.

> I remember the day that postcard came in the mail, I was so thrilled — that it had the stamp from Spain and all that stuff. I still have this postcard. And, you know, it made such an impression on me, that she spent so much time with all of us, that I always wanted to be like her.

Camille, in discussing in-between-the-lines teaching, said she wants children to learn "to care about others and themselves, to want to help someone." Consistently, it was a *disposition* that the participants mentioned, an ethic of care that was admired and remembered. Mary deliberately has birds or animals in her classroom because she believes that children who care for animals have a better chance of growing up to be caring adults. Irene had a principal who sent wonderful notes to teachers, so she does the same with her student teachers.

It is evident that an ethic of care (or its absence) is recognizable, but its manifestation takes many forms. Several of the participants noted that discipline is caring in the sense that a calm, organized classroom contributes to a nurturing environment where children have the best chance to learn. This facet of care has to do with work, responsibility, pride, and self-worth on the part of the students.

> You have to be *real*. You have to be a real person. And you have to care about kids, and I don't mean in this gooey sense. I can't stand that. My discipline is straight from the cuff. I just don't mess around. . . . A lot of learning is very hard work. I want them to get used to — that it's fun, it's hard work, and when you're done, you feel great about it — that "fun" isn't always to sit back and let it flow over you and just happen to you. Fun is being involved and making your mind go round and producing something you're proud of. When they're finished, they're really *proud*. (Amy)

Sometimes, care takes the form of telephoning parents or doing home visits at the beginning of the year to get to know the child from the parent's perspective. As Elizabeth explained, "I want them to know I'm calling because I'm caring about their child." Camille asks parents at the beginning of the year to tell her the strengths and weaknesses of the child and any particular area the parent would like her to work on. As noted earlier, these participants go to great lengths to work with parents. Perhaps the teachers really are *in loco parentis*: As Mary put it, "For an elementary teacher, they are your kids and they never cease to be your kids. When you see them 20 years later, they're still your kids."

Another manifestation of care is the amount of time spent on report card comments "to say what I need to say, but also make it so it's unique for each child." Sometimes it's an "outpouring of care" from colleagues during a difficult time or a principal "forgetting" to report the partial day absence of a teacher who has had to rush to the side of a sick relative. Or it may be community service or fund-raising to help unknown recipients. Occasionally, it is a quiet act of selfless love.

> I had Kelly in elementary school. But it wasn't until she went to middle school and then they moved out of state that I heard that she had a brain tumor. She came back to see me, but unfortunately on that particular day, I was out at a meeting. So I rooted around and I found out the number in [a distant state], and I called up and she was in the hospital so the mother gave me the child's [hospital room] number. So I called her and I talked to her. I would send her tapes 'cause I play the guitar and I played her a couple songs and I talked to her about everything that I thought she might be interested in. Her mother said that when the pain killers weren't working, they would play that tape and it would always bring a smile to her face. (Mary)

Rewards

When teacher rewards are discussed, they are frequently linked to making a difference in children's lives and seeing growth in their students (e.g., Lortie, 1975).

> The other day, the [school] secretary said, "My husband was proofreading the school newsletter for me the other night and he said, 'Who's the teacher in room 16?'" She said, "I told him it was you." (He'd met me at the Christmas party.) And he said, "I like what's going on in her room. I think her room looks like fun for the kids." Just from the newsletter! Now, that's nice. The other reward I like is from the kids. When I see they're enjoying, then I know that I'm doing something that's helping them. And when they're

capable of performing some way or doing something, I feel good about that. (Elizabeth)

Other rewards mentioned by the participants in this study were words and deeds that came from people they respect and rewards linked to the concept of care. If care is a manifestation of respect for individuals, it is possible that all the important rewards, at least for these teachers, are linked to an ethic of care.

A former student wrote me this real sweet letter when she was in fifth grade and I've still got it. I keep certain ones in my pocketbook so that on those days when you think, "Why did I ever get into this?", I pull out those little letters from those kids. One of them — I remember this one that said, "Dear Mrs. Wallace, I love you but please don't tell the rest of the kids." [laugh] So I just keep some of those letters that you get and they do a lot more for me than any award that I could possibly get from anybody 'cause what you're teaching lasts a lifetime. (Mary)

The student teacher that I had last year wrote a letter that recommended me for the award I received. It made me feel wonderful. But the thing that made me feel the most wonderful was the letter. It was — it made me cry and I'm not a weepy sort. The fact that I knew he meant it. That it wasn't flowers and just to do this and butter me up. He wasn't that kind of a person. He was a person that I totally admire. To have him write a letter like that about me really meant a lot. He didn't *have* to. I didn't even know this thing, this award, even existed. He just did this. It was truly out of the kindness of his heart. (Amy)

These teachers related many stories on the same theme. What is important is the meaning and memory associated with this kind of human interaction.

Discussion

As I interviewed the participants, it became clear that caring for other human beings is central to their beliefs about teaching and to their daily practice, yet it is very difficult to describe, in part because it comes in many guises. Above all, however, the participants' caring manifests itself in their attempts to learn to know their students as whole persons. They seem to intuit that knowing someone well may help foster respect for that person, so they involve parents to help give them knowledge of their students and they use collaborative learning so students get to know their peers. They also share of themselves with their students, perhaps drawing on the special relationships five of them had with much respected teachers when they were children.

They recognize that children learn differently and make diverse contributions. They take great care in writing student report cards so each child feels unique. They create a nurturing classroom environment and model what they consider good thinking and behaviors. Their lesson plans are designed to allow for differences in learning and for the intellectual, social, and emotional development of their students.

Since communication and social interactions are the foundation for coming to know, it was no surprise that these teachers work very hard to communicate in various ways that go beyond the classroom: report cards, notes and calls to parents, newsletters, home visits, an open-door policy in their classroom, attention to improving parent/teacher conferences, seeking parent volunteers, careful explanations of curriculum. They also learn a great deal from every possible source and much of their own renewal is directed at improving their teaching to improve their students' learning.

Since so much effort is expended toward student learning and learning about students, the teachers' greatest rewards are in seeing growth and change in their students. The students who come back to see them, the notes from children and parents, unexpected thanks from colleagues they respect — these are the rewards they talk about and remember. These are the rewards that help them through the days when they wonder, "Why did I ever get into this?" This is what gives meaning to their lives, suggesting that if Gardner's (1963/1981) definition of commitment is accepted, an ethic of care is strongly connected to the participants' commitment to teaching.

Commitment

Renewal assists teachers, by encouraging them and giving them strength to continue their professional efforts. . . . But renewal is by its nature personal, and the restoration of confidence and skill and commitment and energy varies dramatically from teacher to teacher.
                                        Rud and Oldendorf (1992, pp. 2-3)

Gardner (1963/1981) referred to commitment as the motivation to do something about which one cares deeply and as a happiness grounded in "striving toward meaningful goals — goals that relate the individual to a larger context of purposes. . . . conceptions of the universe that give dignity, purpose and sense to our own existence" (pp. 97; 102). It is evident that the participants perceive learning and caring to be vitally important for themselves and others and that their satisfaction is linked to that belief. Their drive to improve their own learning in order to make a social contribution appears to be associated with the work ethic they learned as children. And, as described earlier, their broadening scope of professional awareness and involvement contributed to their increasingly global perspective of education.

Decisions about Teaching

The participants' decisions to become a teacher and stay in the profession may also shed light on the difficult concept of commitment. Mary, Camille, and Donna had always had teaching in mind as a career. Donna still has a childhood composition on wanting to be a teacher, although at the beginning of college, she briefly toyed with the idea of being a psychologist because of the prestige and money she associated with it. Amy considered being a pharmacist, psychiatrist, or psychologist but thought she didn't have an adequate science background. Irene and Elizabeth thought of becoming a nurse, but the required math and science made them change their mind as well. It should be noted that, except for Donna, the other five teachers entered college during the historical period when the main jobs for women were perceived to be teaching, nursing, or secretarial.

Camille has always felt most comfortable and able to do her best as a teacher. Donna also sees herself staying in education, although she envisions herself trying different roles. However, the decision to teach does not necessarily indicate that commitment cannot be broken. For Elizabeth, the crisis came swiftly and harshly.

> The first year I taught, the first semester was very difficult and I went on a vacation to New York with two other first year teachers for Christmas vacation. We just cried and cried and went to see plays and spent money and ate, and came back and said, "Those kids are *not* gettin' to me! I don't care what happens. I'm not going to let a twelve-year-old defeat me!" The rest of the year, what I did was try to figure out, "How could I make the room better?" Other than that, I never really thought about leaving teaching at all [despite being offered two other jobs].

For Irene and Amy, there were two affirmations to stay in teaching, even though at that time, they viewed teaching as a job, not a career. The first was made in their second year of teaching and the second after the birth of a child. For her second assignment, Irene was transferred to a school whose principal and staff embodied everything she could not accept: teachers who did not work together, teachers who slammed doors and yelled at children, and a principal who did not believe all children can learn. But having worked so hard at her job and in her classes to get through college, she refused to be beaten. She said to herself, "No one's going to kick me out of here. I'm going to quit when I'm ready. I'm not giving up!" After the birth of her first child several years later, she realized that she wanted to go back to teaching and does not see herself leaving education.

Amy was in an inner city school during racial riots and, besides feeling unsafe, hated having to be on a certain page of the manual by a given day. Although three of the five new teachers in that school did not finish the year, she did not want to break her contract.

> It wasn't teaching and I *knew* that wasn't teaching; it was surviving. I was more of a policeman than anything. That was *not* the way I intended to continue my educational career! I was looking to the corporate world and was headed out.

But when she moved to a different state that summer, she chose a teaching position despite having had two corporate job offers. Nevertheless, when she became pregnant, she handed in her resignation papers, thinking she would stay home. It was shortlived.

> I just started rethinking it [pause] because *I* needed to work. For my *own* self. And so I pulled it back [her resignation letter] and the board just reinstated me. And I think because I always felt my mother was so short-changed in life, I think it sent me back into the workforce right away. That was a good decision.

Mary came close to leaving the profession in her ninth year. Having always loved teaching and her students, she was stunned to be wrongfully accused of slapping a child. That was followed by anonymous phone calls to the principal accusing Mary of abuse. She almost cracked under the weight of having her integrity shattered.

> I'll tell you, my heart — I mean, my heart was *way* down. It was a very very very very hard year. I was very close to getting out, very close because it wasn't any fun anymore and I felt that I couldn't teach because I was so worried [that] if I hugged a kid, would I be accused of molestation or what? If I separated kids that were fighting would I be — I would always be second guessing. I came very close that year. Very, very close. My husband was very, very supportive. He said, "Whatever you do, I'm behind you." And I thought, "Well, I will last through this year." And I did. . . but then I really got angry. I got *angry* and it was like, "You're not going to throw *me* out of teaching." It really got my dander up. But I think there is a wariness in me now.

126

Mary's story again links care and commitment.

Discussion

In the literature, particularly organizational theory, commitment has typically been linked to extrinsic rewards and/or school goals. The definition by Reyes (1990) is representative: Teacher commitment is "a psychological identification of the individual with the school's goals and values, and the intention of that teacher to maintain organizational membership and become involved in the job beyond personal interest" (pp. 153-154). Commitment is a "willingness on the teacher's part to exert extra effort on behalf of the schools to make it effective that goes beyond the individual's interest" (p. 304).

This study suggests, however, that while rewards are meaningful and congruency of school and individual beliefs is very important, the concept of commitment and motivation contributing to commitment may be much more complex. The teachers' search for knowledge and positive social relationships were the driving force behind their increasingly expanding scope of their interest and involvement, from the classroom to the school, from the district to beyond. What needs to be studied further is what teachers do to transcend classroom isolation (Lortie, 1975) and infantilization (Huberman, 1993). Physical walls did not stop these teachers from teaching, learning, and interacting beyond the classroom or the school. It may be that closing physical classroom doors closes out learning and human interaction, cutting off possibilities for the global kind of commitment Gardner (1963/1981) believed vital to human beings: a "striving toward meaningful goals — goals that relate the individual to a larger context of purposes . . . . conceptions of the universe that give dignity, purpose and sense to our own existence" (pp. 97; 102). I suspect that meaning in life is not possible without fruitful interactions with other human beings.

Although the teachers talked about decisions they had to make to stay in teaching, the data do not explain what it was that made some angry enough to stay instead of leaving teaching. What the data do appear to establish is a connection between learning, social interaction, and commitment. Because these three characteristics are the major attributes ascribed to exemplary teachers, there appears to be a supported basis on which to argue that we must attend to all three if we want to foster exemplary teachers in our schools.

Ideal Visions for Teachers' Professional Development

Research question: What are exemplary teachers' visions for improving professional development for teachers?

Each participant was asked to describe their ideal vision for improving professional development for teachers. Many of the suggestions reflect the participants' perceptions of what was most valuable to them. Many focus on preservice education and the beginning years of teaching. Camille summed up the participants' belief that if good habits are set early, the teachers have a solid foundation on which to build and the habits a greater likelihood of enduring. What follows is a compilation of their ideas, many of which were suggested by all of the participants:

1. concern that cooperating or associate teachers need to be selected with greater care; (Suggestions included "someone who is successful with the children, has a good attitude toward teaching, someone who is still thrilled about teaching, someone who can be flexible knowing that this student teacher is going to have some moments that are going to be flops, someone willing to take a risk, teachers who voluntarily sign up to go to workshops, someone recommended by teachers in the building.")
2. student teaching lasting the entire year;
3. a year of internship or being an assistant teacher placed with a mentor teacher; (It was noted that there would need to be time — not always after school — for talking with the mentor; getting together with other new teachers; having inservice training on the resources, curriculum, and policies of the district; and visiting other classrooms or schools.)
4. the opportunity for teachers to team teach very early in their career;
5. reading professional literature and attending conferences right away, perhaps with one journal subscription and one conference per year;
6. reading recovery training after several years in the classroom;
7. role playing and observing veteran teachers in order to learn how to do parent/teacher conferences well; (The main idea here was to learn diplomacy, key phrases and questions, and accentuation of the child's progress. It was also noted that learning to read non-verbal clues of parents and to recognize pleas for help that are hidden in "ordinary" questions or statements is a necessary skill.)
8. observation with honest feedback or analysis from respected colleagues;
9. small discussion groups to share ideas and new research;
10. flexible time and sabbaticals;
11. encouragement to attend conferences;
12. assistance in how to work with parents and volunteers;
13. practice in writing curriculum; (It was suggested that new teachers begin by working on and sharing units, then being involved in division planning, and also working on writing teams. What was emphasized was the need to understand the process involved.)

14. grade transfers in order to stay creative and to understand children's development as well as curriculum scope and sequence;
15. term appointments of administrative and resource positions so that people rotate back into classrooms; (Coupled with this was a call for much more careful and stringent selection for leadership roles.

> I would never just take *one* method of determining: It would have to [include] certain guidelines; there would have to be an interview; it would have to be teacher input, principal input; it would have to be people coming in and watching you in the classroom with a set of criteria that they're looking for. They would have to actually watch you dealing with a class several times. I think it should be over a whole year. Look at the type of planning you do. How you implement it. How do you assess? How do you keep records? How do you talk about kids? It would have to be a long [process]. It would almost have to be that long involved personal portfolio kind of accumulation of teachers before you decide on who would be good in that role. If you would insist on a personal portfolio of experiences with students, it would weed out those people immediately that have no business being there.)

16. a resource teacher in each school so follow-up and implementation of innovations can be assisted. (The resource person would be available to model innovations or follow up inservice presentations in whatever way the teachers required depending on their own expertise. This person would model teach, or help teachers plan or analyze their lessons, or free a teacher for observation in a different classroom. This was not viewed as remedial help in any way; innovations and discussions would be expected of *all* teachers. It was also noted that the position would be a term appointment and would require great support from the principal and district.)

Discussion

The ideal vision for professional development outlined by the participants reflects the experiences they experienced and valued most throughout their own careers to date. They put strong emphasis on the importance of observation, analysis, and genuine feedback as a tool for improving teaching/learning. They clearly believe that becoming an exemplary teacher is a difficult and unending process of "becoming," a process that requires the assistance of many other colleagues.

Their concern with the selection of teachers in leadership roles, coupled with the stories of their own renewal, indicates that they did not have enough exemplary leaders or mentors encouraging them to stretch their wings and fly. They have managed to pursue self-renewal and have relied hugely on their extensive collegial networks to find meaningful opportunities to learn. However, they suggest that without the help of colleagues who have the knowledge and desire to assist other teachers, an already challenging pursuit is made unnecessarily more difficult.

Summary

This chapter introduced the six teacher participants and elaborated their formative experiences, preservice teacher education, common experiences as beginning teachers, and beliefs about teaching and learning. Personal and professional renewal, as well as selected factors enabling and/or constraining their renewal, were discussed. Finally, the importance of care and commitment in their lives was portrayed and their ideal visions for professional development described. Chapter 5 outlines several implications of the study and suggests areas for further research.

CHAPTER V
IMPLICATIONS AND SUGGESTIONS FOR FUTURE RESEARCH

Throughout the study, I have indicated that the participants in this inquiry reveal dispositions that are strikingly similar to those in Gardner's (1963/1981) conceptualization of self-renewing individuals. I submit that the participants in this study are able to adapt to change and succeed in the uncertain, complex world of schools because they have learned how to be self-renewing individuals. What this investigation clearly reveals is that their journey toward exemplary teaching and continuous professional renewal has been supported in large measure by:

1. a *disposition* to question, reflect, seek alternatives, weigh consequences, and move toward increasingly good judgment. This allows them to analyze their work and to use their knowledge and resources (often their network of colleagues) to find other possible approaches to try to solve problems and help children learn in individual ways.
2. their *knowledge* of children, curriculum, the workplace, and the community. They alter, ignore, challenge, or adapt curriculum to their context and to what they think will help the group of students they have at the time. Rather than taking a passive role, they get involved on curriculum writing committees, negotiating teams, promotion/retention committees — any role that allows them to voice their opinion or that offers a modicum of influence on their primary concern: teaching children in the best possible ways they can find.
3. a deep *belief* that education is important and that as teachers, they can make a difference in the lives of some children. They are not unrealistic about what they as an individual can accomplish, but as one participant put it, they "believe in small miracles." Those small miracles sustain and give meaning to the lives of these teachers.

4. an appreciation of the whole educational *community* — classroom teachers, parents as teachers, teacher educators, and researchers — as resources for and contributors to children's and adults' learning;
5. an explicit set of *ethics* they have come to value and that they teach to their students.

Of the many implications resulting from this study, I have selected three major areas for discussion. They include implications for including teachers' dispositions and biographies as a specific focus in teacher selection; implications for designing teacher education to foster dispositions of self-renewing individuals and encourage experiences that the participants found to be valuable contributors to their professional growth; and implications for structuring desirable contexts to support continuous professional renewal of teachers.

Teacher Selection

An Argument for Academic Ability *and* Dispositions

For many years, we have been relying on academic grades and standardized tests to define "academically able" students. However, a synthesis of survey research (Walberg, 1990) indicates that educators, parents, and students, when given a choice, rank nonstandard outcomes "far above standardized test achievements and grades" (p. 291). Nonstandard outcomes include areas such as cooperation, critical thinking, self-reliance, constructive attitudes, and lifelong learning. Walberg points out that these outcomes were the ideals of open education programs which generally emphasized the role of the child in learning, diagnostic instead of norm-referenced evaluation, individualized instruction, and manipulative materials. Open education was also associated with multi-age groups, open space, and team teaching. In a second synthesis of research studies, open classes appeared to "enhance several nonstandard outcomes without detracting from academic achievement, unless they are radically extreme" (p. 292).

It may be that open educational settings attract teachers with a strong disposition to learn and to have fruitful relations with others. It is reasonable to assume that the teachers would have to have developed these dispositions to some degree themselves in order to teach or model them to children. Since a love of learning and fruitful relations with others (as well as some of the other non-standard outcomes) are descriptive of self-renewing individuals and exemplary teachers, it does not seem accidental that the participants in this study enjoyed teaching/learning in open space settings early in their careers and that they continue to value nonstandard outcomes and support similar environments with or without physical walls. It is likely that exemplary teachers have been teaching these dispositions all along, but as Dewey

(1899/1976) argued, we cannot leave the teaching of dispositions to chance. If self-renewing individuals are desirable, then we need to foster and support related dispositions in teachers.

Also built on the assumptions of academically able is the argument that college students in education typically are less able in the sense that they are drawn from the lower academic quartiles (Schlechty and Vance, 1983). Four of the participants attained "A" averages from elementary school through college. Despite an "A" average, when Amy took the ACT (American College Test), she was counselled out of teaching because of her poor test score. Irene was counselled out of teaching because of her low results in high school. She recalls being bored with school until she began her education program in her third year. Her interest soared and she finished college with a 3.4 GPA (Grade Point Average), an average that included two years of low college grades.

Elizabeth also enjoyed education courses following a disastrous year of science courses and commented on her new-found motivation: "I had a 3.8 [GPA] when I graduated 'cause once I got into the professional school and I was taking education courses, I was taking courses I really worked for." Nor did the participants abandon formal education: Five completed their Master's degrees or beyond with high levels of achievement and the sixth is currently working on a Master's degree. Four considered enrolling in a doctoral program.

Given the priority of continuous learning, care, and commitment in the lives of these teachers, I submit that in selecting education as a career, they may have seen possibilities of encouraging and enhancing in others what they believe to be important and what they live by example. From their parents, or teachers they admired, or by means of their imagination, they envisioned teaching as meaningful, interesting, and important work (though not necessarily recognized as such by the public). They learned dispositions they came to value and they saw teaching as a way to make a difference in children's lives.

Use of Teachers' Dispositions and Biographies in Teacher Selection

I am not implying that academic ability be abandoned as a criterion in selecting teachers, but the results of this study emphasize that exemplary teaching requires much more than academic ability. What is valued is a set of dispositions with the potential to enable teachers to become exemplary. I am recommending that these dispositions be made explicit and incorporated into selection criteria.

Teachers' dispositions

Since academic grades alone do not reflect dispositions nor indicate future exemplary teachers, the inclusion of dispositions as a specific focus of the selection or screening process would at least broaden many present methods of selecting teacher candidates, hiring teachers, and selecting teacher leaders and teacher educators. Teaching dispositions along with academics is not a new concept; Dewey, for example, advocated teaching dispositions throughout his career. However, it is an area that has not been examined or researched extensively and, with few exceptions (e.g., Howey and Strom, 1987), has not been an explicit part of teacher education.

It is the business community that is currently calling for graduates who not only are academically able, but who also are dependable, creative, innovative problem solvers, able to work with colleagues, and the like. This is a move away from reliance on the standards of academically able and redefines what "an educated person" is. The participants in this study came to similar conclusions some time ago and welcome philosophy and practice in this direction.

For example, the recent interest in teacher outcomes and outcomes-based education in several instances is an attempt to define and include dispositions as an explicit part of teaching/learning (e.g., INTASC, 1992; NASDTEC, 1992). The inclusion of problem solving and critical thinking into the curriculum may reflect the same trend. This tendency raises several questions:

1. If non-standard outcomes or dispositions are valued by at least some teachers, have they taught these to children whether the outcomes are explicit or not? If so, in what manner?
2. Do open, healthy schools or learning enriched schools encourage and make explicit the teaching of certain dispositions? If so, in what specific ways?
3. If a community agrees on certain outcomes or dispositions as valuable, what enabling experiences in teacher education would assist teachers to teach more than academics?

Thus, I suggest that further research into how dispositions are learned is needed (see Howey and Strom, 1987, on how to determine and assess dispositions). Better understanding of how we acquire dispositions could also yield information that parents would find helpful: Their role as teachers of children could be enhanced with a clearer explanation of how dispositions are learned and specific examples of how they can model and encourage desired dispositions.

Teachers' biographies

Throughout the interviews, the participants illustrated the dispositions Gardner (1963/1981) detailed in describing self-renewing individuals. The question is, how did they learn these dispositions? Although further research in this area is required, there were some clues in the teachers' stories. The participants talked about learning *a work ethic* from their parents: not only to do their best at what they consider important work, but also to pursue ways to "make things better" (continuous improvement). The notion of seeking alternative possibilities has been learned as well and they draw on any available source to succeed in teaching, solve problems, or make decisions.

Additionally, the teachers talked about how observant children are and how important *observation* is to them as adult learners. They credit their early experiences in team teaching with engendering a habit of seeking new ideas and self-monitoring their behavior. One participant commented that new teachers are unlikely to envision what better teaching can be unless they observe other teachers in action. All of the teachers commented on the importance of *reflection* in improving their teaching; the two who had specific training emphasizing reflection now ask for their students' reflections as one way of improving their teaching. At the same time, they know that they are also teaching their students a habit of thinking that they personally have found to be a valuable, lifelong learning strategy.

When the participants were discussing in-between-the-lines teaching, they talked about the importance of *modelling* desirable behaviors, values, and dispositions: problem solving, human relations, diversity, love of learning, risk taking, reflection, caring, self-reliance. As for modelling they had observed as children, they commented on significant adults, particularly teachers, they had learned from and now try to emulate. These exemplary teachers are well aware that they teach the dispositions they value along with the academic curriculum.

Some of the participants had an image of themselves as teachers years before the fact. All perceive emphatically that they are not "traditional" teachers. By traditional, they mean that an almost exclusive emphasis is put on academics and "covering the curriculum." From their early experiences as students or young teachers, they all saw or created pedagogical approaches that appealed to them much more.

The participants' biographies indicate that the dispositions they learned have helped them to work successfully in the complex, uncertain, constantly changing realm of a profession dependent on social interactions. We may for years have made serious errors in judgment by accepting preservice candidates almost exclusively on the basis of academic ability. Further study of teachers' biographies (e.g., patterns of involvement, social skills, dispositions, and their resulting beliefs about teaching/learning) may uncover significant clues concerning success in teaching and habits of self-renewal.

Teacher "image" and early success in teaching
Only Elizabeth mentioned having a difficult introduction to teaching and it was shortlived. This is quite different from the career stage theories concerning beginning teachers (see Christensen, 1985). There may be partial explanations within the

teachers' biographies. For example, Elizabeth is the only participant who did not decide to be a teacher until her third year of college; she had always pictured herself as a nurse. Nor is she one of the four teachers who had extended preservice time in classrooms for observation and teaching. Nevertheless, she did participate in Future Teachers of America in highschool and was often asked to "take over the class."

I suspect that there may be a connection between the early success of these participants and the length of time they had to create and become comfortable with an image of themselves as teachers. Further research of teachers' biographies may indicate whether teachers' degree of success in their initial teaching year is linked to the timing of their decision to become a teacher. If so, some preservice teachers may need more time to be in schools and to practice teach than their regular program provides. Flexible exit dates from preservice teaching might be helpful.

Teachers as recruiting agents

As Lortie (1975) pointed out, children have years and years over which to observe teachers. Five of the participants vividly recalled some wonderful teachers and three specifically linked what they do in their own classrooms with what they learned from those teachers. Through extracurricular activities, they learned to see and know those teachers differently — as a person with a life and personality outside the classroom. I suspect that few classroom teachers see themselves as "recruiting agents" for future teachers, but they may well have a student who, because of them, decides for or against teaching as a career choice. Given that some students decide to be teachers when they are very young, *all* teachers need to work toward becoming exemplary and to consider their role in vocational counselling. Further, if children articulate their desire to become a teacher, they should be encouraged to help the teacher in tasks like reading to a group or explaining an assignment so that their image of themselves as a teacher is supported with success.

Teacher Education

A Focus on What Teachers Need to Learn

When the participants referred to experiences of team teaching in an open space, reading recovery training, and a resource leadership role as their "real education," what specific teaching/learning made the experiences so stimulating and powerful? I suggest that their experiences laid the foundation for successful teaching and strengthened their disposition for inquiry. Over a prolonged period of time with their team mates, the participants learned:

1. to be constantly aware of what they are saying and doing and how that is fostering learning;

2. to feel at ease being observed by peers or other adults and to use their observation and feedback as a learning tool;

3. to understand that teaching/learning is collaborative and that ideas and support can come from many sources;

4. to learn the art of giving and receiving criticism *with a view to improving practice*;

5. to keep learning about the theories and research (with their accompanying vocabulary) that undergird teaching;

6. to use appropriate terminology and evidence to support or discuss one's position.

Working with peers, the participants came to recognize and appreciate diversity and the strengths of their partners; that is, that there are many perspectives and many effective solutions and ways of teaching. Working together fostered a sense of community, tolerance, and respect for each other as they examined their beliefs in light of others' positions. They saw everything and everyone as a resource. Above all, having other adult eyes and ears nearby engendered a habit of "reading behavior" and monitoring how they treat children.

The participants recognized that knowledge and vocabulary, which were included in the theoretical component of their training, are important to improving their teaching/learning. Dewey (1904/1965) argued that theory must be balanced with practice right from the beginning of a teacher's career and that knowledge and specialized language are associated with reflection (Dewey, 1933/1960; Fosnot, 1989; Schon, 1987). Simmons and Schuette (1988) concluded that "[w]ithout such precise pedagogical language and concepts, reflective decision-making is rendered much more primitive or even impossible" (p. 21). If inquiry (including reflection) and theory (including knowledge and its specialized vocabulary) result in the exhilarating learning several of the participants claimed, then they must systematically be incorporated into teacher education over a long period of time.

Inquiry and human interaction as a focus of teacher education

Some preservice programs are already recognizing the value of having teachers get to know each other well over a prolonged period of time; their preservice teachers are organized into cohorts.

To allow preservice teachers to be in the schools as much as possible and to support discussion and analysis of practice, I suggest a university/school partnership similar to the idea of Professional Development Schools, but with a somewhat different division of teaching responsibilities. I propose that schools with carefully selected and trained cohorts of exemplary cooperative teachers be responsible for all of the "practical" part of teaching. Ideally, the schools would have teams of exemplary teachers already in place. The university and cooperating teachers would work closely together so agreed upon goals and desirable dispositions could be reinforced in each locale. The teachers would be trained to foster inquiry and to design questions for joint analysis and critique of lessons team taught by colleagues and preservice teachers.

To analyze a lesson, the team might use questions such as:

1. What were the main strengths of the lesson/activity?
2. What pre-planning was required?
3. What specific strategies were used? With what results?
4. What did not work? Why not?
5. What alternative approaches could have been used? What might the consequences have been?
6. What teacher beliefs were apparent? What evidence supports your conclusions?

This set of repeated questions would be an attempt to teach the preservice teachers to self-monitor prior to teaching a lesson.

Groups of cooperating teachers could also work together to help their preservice teachers with analysis of and phrases to look for in observing role played or real parent/teacher conferences. They could plan for examination of the scope and sequence of curriculum, observation of children, practice in writing anecdotal report cards, the articulation of reflection, discipline, parental involvement, and the like.

The role of the university would be to assist cohorts of preservice teachers in areas that improve teaching, but are less likely to be best carried out in schools (e.g., public speaking skills, theoretical development, cognitive development). The university work could nevertheless be linked to observations and practices in the schools. Teaching requires speaking skills, so the university section could include persuasive public speaking. For example, Tatum's (1993) work on communication and feedback evaluation might act as a model for designing specific skills and precise evaluation questions. The preservice teachers could then work with their cooperating teachers to reinforce the skills in the classroom.

The university could design and teach courses in human relations that preservice teachers could then practice in the schools. They might use video or audio clips or journals as follow-up reflection about their own development. Preservice teachers could also observe a video clip of a lesson and go through the above set of questions, but the instructor could then link what was observed with current research or theoretical underpinnings, thus incorporating specialized knowledge and vocabulary. Additionally, the university could work with instruments or devices that enhance specific dispositions like creativity (e.g., Samson, 1965) or areas like cognitive development (see Howey and Strom, 1987, for examples) so that preservice teachers would have a personal exit portfolio that could be used as part of the teacher selection process. They would also have a professional portfolio compiled at the school site.

Inservice teacher education

Rosenholtz (1989) made a statement that seems obvious in its simplicity: "Common sense suggests that people engaged in the process of educating others should also be allowed their own learning, critical inquiry, and debate. Those with limited opportunity for professional growth are not only ill-equipped for an inherently changing environment, but they unwittingly become programmed for sameness and routine, exacting costs of incalculable proportion" (p. 217). Yet despite arguments and models for career-long education for teachers (e.g., Burke and Heideman, 1985; Dewey, 1899/1976), it is not a common expectation for teachers.

Part of the difficulty of designing continuous inservice education may be that districts have not made explicit their expectations of the kind of teacher one can work toward becoming over time. If the dispositions of self-renewing individuals were selected, then professional development could be planned to assist teachers in engaging in *inquiry* with a view to its becoming a habit, moving on a continuum from preference to *supported judgment*, and increasing skills in *human relations*.

Dewey (1899/1976) was keenly aware that learning needs to be directed instead of haphazard if it is to be educative and enriching (pp. 24-28). He envisioned education as a transformation from interest to discipline and knowledge, or as Chambers (1983) explained, a transformation from occurrent interest to dispositional interest. "The formation of habits is a purely mechanical thing unless habits are also *tastes* — habitual modes of preference and esteem, an effective sense of excellence" (Dewey, 1916/1966, p. 102). "[T]he question of education is the question of taking hold of [learners'] activities, of giving them direction. Through direction, through organized use, they tend toward valuable results, instead of scattering or being left to merely impulsive expression" (Dewey, 1899/1976, p. 25).

If this study is representative of teachers' professional self-renewal, my impression is that their renewal activities do risk being haphazard and limited by time, availability of opportunities in areas like research, access to information, and the inability to extend their learning beyond a given point without the intervention of a person who has more expertise or knowledge in a particular area. For example, districts might want all of their teachers within the first five years of their career to have further training in technology or multiculturalism. The district could work with the university and available expertise in the community to design courses or seminars. Or districts could facilitate and disseminate periodic lists of helpful books that teachers, professors, parents, or librarians have found. Not only would the wider community be focussing on education, but the district would be clarifying expectations.

If a district selected a specific framework for professional development (e.g., Howey's expanded imperative, 1985), the university could help to develop a balanced program based on assessments from teachers and the district. If, as the data in this study suggest, pedagogical development is already handled well among teachers, it could be left to the district. In the area of research, university personnel could offer a seminar where a cohort of inservice teachers might decide to explore an area like teacher questioning in the classroom. The teachers could be directed to background reading and discussion in the seminar, but would then go back into their classrooms to tape lessons and collect data on their questioning and on student responses. Discussion and analysis of the data in the seminar could lead to suggestions for improvement, prompting further examination in the classroom to determine whether the suggested alternatives elicited fuller, more thoughtful responses from students.

In this study, much of the renewal teachers sought, particularly theoretical development, was specifically undertaken in order to find explanations and support for their practices. Cohorts of veteran teachers could view a video clip of a lesson/ activity one had taught and then, with the help of each other and the instructor, analyze what beliefs and assumptions guide their practice. The teachers might also be asked to explain the theoretical and philosophical underpinning of the district's policy related to a unit they have designed. Or the university might offer refresher courses on contemporary issues, recent research in areas such as expert/novice thinking, ethics, national trends and reforms, and so forth as a way for teachers to try to stay up to date. Ideally, the district would set expectations for regular updating by teachers and support it with release time and a funding formula.

Creating Desirable Contexts for Self-Renewal

Working from the participants' beliefs about teaching/learning and their desire to create nurturing classrooms to help children grow toward self-reliance and independence, schools too must move toward providing a similar environment for teachers as learners. Time has not dulled the urgency of Dewey's (1916/1966) observation: "[L]ife means growth . . . . [and] education means the enterprise of supplying the conditions which ensure growth, or adequacy of life, irrespective of age" (p. 51).

The participants share Yee's (1990) conclusion that veteran teachers who have decided to make teaching a career value professional growth opportunities and challenges that include "collegial exchange, opportunities to take on additional roles and to participate in decisions. . . . They want to exercise some control over what matters most to them — student learning" (pp. 114-115). Though collegiality is not well understood, it was of utmost importance to these participants. Team teaching in an open space seems to be the best environment for helping teachers get to know and respect each other. Failing that, schools can arrange staff retreats and set up ongoing, regular small group discussions that deal with substantive issues.

Expectations and an overarching school philosophy can be determined by the staff and made explicit when interviewing for new team members. There could also be an explicit expectation that, over time, teachers would expand their knowledge of and/or scope of involvement beyond the school. Internal classroom coverage might be arranged on a rotating basis so staff members could observe other teachers or attend conferences and then come back and lead a discussion of what they learned and its connection to practice.

The participants painted a very clear picture of what professionalism means to them and its importance to their work. Articulation of what professionalism means to individual teachers could be a step towards examining staff expectations, behaviors, and tacit beliefs. Further, the participants were clear about wanting to be treated as professional equals and to be "allowed" to express opinions, disagree, and give and hear reasons and justifications for decisions. Their reactions are similar to comments by Cohn (1992) in a study on how teachers perceive teaching.

> Collegial endeavors in education cannot easily occur without all the various constituencies in direct and open communication. Depending on the particular arrangement, this may mean that teachers must be able to speak honestly to each other as well as to principals, superintendents, and board members without fear of reprisal. It may mean that principals and superintendents must be able to share power and learn to operate within new parameters with teachers, parents, students, and community members. . . . But with increased participation also comes the probability of genuine differences and disagreements." (p. 134)

Gardner (1963/1981) argued that democracy is a necessary condition for self-renewal. Democratic ideals include liberty (the disciplining of power and the dispersal of power), regard for the worth of the individual, and pluralism (many decision points rather than only one, a willingness to entertain diverse views, access to multiple ways of knowing and expressing those views) (pp. xv; 67). From these flow the ideals of equity, justice, responsibility, and consequences. The teachers' comments suggest that personal and professional maturity and renewal can only flourish when democratic ideals are respected and practiced. Examining the school as a democracy-in-action, perhaps guided by a skilled outside person, could lead to an honest discussion of what such a school would be like and the responsibilities required of all members to help it flourish and to sustain learning by children and teachers.

Suggestions for Further Research

Exemplary Teachers

Gardner (1963/1981), like others, recognized that continuous learning and human relations are necessary for self-renewal. Learning, generally associated with the intellect, and care, frequently linked to the emotional, are intertwined in Gardner's conceptualization. An argument for cognitive/emotions association has more recently been made by Scheffler (1991). Similarly, Sherman (1989) has used Aristotle's theory of virtue to argue that practical reason and the sentiments together constitute character. She points out how learning any ethic is really inquiry: Exceptions to our accumulation of patterns prompt puzzlement, questioning, possibilities, judgments, and justification. "[T]he goal is . . . to prepare the learner for eventually arriving at competent judgements and reactions on his own" (p. 172). The process parallels the inquiry process or intellectual posture described by Dewey (1933/1960) and advocated by Gardner (1963/1981).

It would seem then that exemplary teachers' continuous learning includes both intellectual and ethical inquiry. Are exemplary teachers recognized as such because they continuously inquire? Because they have learned a great deal in *both* intellectual and ethical domains? Because they teach their students through inquiry? Because they teach ethics (in-between-the-lines teaching) along with the course of study? Because they have learned to articulate beliefs and practices? Thus, we need to inquire more into what exemplary teachers see as teaching.

Further research is also needed to answer other questions this study generated. For example, is there a consistent image of exemplary teachers across international borders? Would the participants' beliefs about teaching/learning and their ethics be consistent with a random sample of the district's teachers or with a sample of exemplary teachers in a different district? Through sustained observation, can we better understand how teachers teach dispositions and ethics? Would the common experiences of the participants in this study (e.g., team teaching, observation, open space) be similar to early career experiences of another sample of teachers nominated as exemplary? Is their definition of professionalism and their portrait of an exemplary principal similar to or different from other teachers' views? Is a desire to teach adults (e.g., through leadership roles) part of a broadening scope of involvement?

I would like to replicate this study in other urban settings and include minority groups (gender and race) within the elementary school teacher population. Comparisons could also be made with case studies of teachers nominated as exemplary in suburban and rural settings.

This type of study also lends itself to issues related to gender, issues such as: the participants' lack of confidence and learning in math and science; career decisions; the impact of family on their renewal; choices they have made; ways of knowing; and preferred styles of leadership in administrators and for themselves.

Teacher Commitment and Retention

Finally, this study raised a profusion of questions about commitment to teaching, an area that seems as difficult to understand as collegiality. How does commitment manifest itself? In this study, what role did anger play when the participants faced the possibility of leaving teaching? Did pride in their work influence their decisions to re-commit to teaching?

The data from this study indicate that commitment seems to be associated with learning opportunities, human interactions, one's work ethic, rewards, professional confidence, the workplace environment, the teacher's scope of involvement in the educational arena, and issues of power and task autonomy. Further research is needed to find out how some or all of these (and perhaps additional) factors are associated with commitment. Naturalistic research on teachers' decisions to transfer to and from schools, decisions by exemplary teachers who stayed in teaching, and decisions of those who chose to leave teaching could also contribute to our understanding of commitment.

Conclusion

The purpose of this study was to broaden our understanding of how exemplary teachers engage in renewal throughout their careers, their beliefs about teaching/learning, and the nature of the contexts that best support exemplary teachers and teacher renewal. The data indicate to me that exemplary teachers have a wealth of knowledge and perceptive insight. They are a rich resource with much to teach us about teaching/learning, beliefs and dispositions, caring and commitment, and personal and professional renewal. This investigation reinforced the idea that the role of teachers within organizations is complex and that their renewal is mediated by a multiplicity of both organizational and personal factors.

The study has indicated specific areas for further inquiry, such as the process of becoming an exemplary teacher, the role of teacher education in fostering dispositions, and the complex questions concerning teacher commitment. It has also signalled directions for needed improvements in the selection and preparation of teachers as well as the contexts in which they work.

APPENDIX A

NOMINATION FORM

Besides being exemplary teachers, nominees should also:

1. be female classroom teachers in an elementary school;

2. have at least 10 years experience;

3. intend to continue as classroom teachers (i.e., not someone who will be an administrator in September).

Teacher's Full Name	School	Tel No. (school)	Tel. No. (home)

Would you please briefly list criteria you used in selecting these teachers as exemplary.

Vivienne Collinson
Doctoral Candidate
The Ohio State University

APPENDIX B

GUIDED INTERVIEW SCHEDULES

GUIDED INTERVIEW 1

DATE:

I. **Personal**

    A.   <u>Family</u>
        1.   responsibilities
        2.   support
        3.   changing priorities over career

    B.   <u>Academic Background</u>
        1.   family's emphasis on education
        2.   academic achievements
        3.   salient experiences at school/college
        4.   outstanding teacher models
        5.   why teaching selected as a career

    C.   <u>Personal Renewal</u>
        1.   community involvement or leadership
        2.   interests and pursuits
        3.   their influence or effect within the school
        4.   enabling/constraining factors affecting renewal

GUIDED INTERVIEW 2

DATE:

II. **Professional**

A.   <u>Professional Renewal</u>
        1.   kinds of professional development activities
        2.   patterns of scope of interest and involvement
             (e.g., school based, district, state, national)
        3.   collegial relationships/networks

B.   Organizational Climate
           1.   enabling/constraining factors affecting renewal
                  - relationship with principal
                  - organization of school
                  - resources
                  - collegiality
                  - parents and community
                  - curriculum
                  - school/district support for renewal
                  - decision making processes
                  - student achievement
           2.   OCDQ-RE Questionnaire

INTERVIEW 3

DATE:

III.   **Personal and Professional**

     A.   Beliefs and Perceptions
           1.   beliefs about learning and teaching
           2.   decisions surrounding staying in/leaving teaching
           3.   how constraints are handled
           4.   impact of personal and professional renewal on teaching
           5.   vision of an ideal professional development model

APPENDIX C

PROFESSIONAL DEVELOPMENT ACTIVITIES

FOR TEACHERS

- professional conversations/discussions (Yonemura, 1982)
- visiting other classrooms
- reading
- reviewing teaching on videotape
- conferences
- inservice training (after school, on P. D. days, or on release time)
- self-evaluation
- being involved in a program review
- taking formal courses
- experimenting in classroom
- mentoring new teachers or teachers new to grade level (Thies-Sprinthall & Sprinthall, 1987)
- being a cooperating/associate teacher (training preservice teachers)
- having visitors to the classroom
- committee work (school or district level)
- curriculum writing
- sabbaticals
- living with another professional: share techniques and be a reality check
- talking to parents
- having parent volunteers
- using community resource personnel (observing their techniques and professional skill)
- working with good, open leaders
- team teaching
- being asked for advice
- clinical faculty member (Thies-Sprinthall & Sprinthall, 1987)
- presenting workshops
- chairing meetings
- writing proposals
- peer coaching (Joyce & Showers, 1980)
- parent/teacher conferences
- curricular innovations
- new instructional techniques
- professional organizations/memberships

- community service/organizations
- collegial networks
- writing for publication
- self-initiated or requested ideas (e.g., designing interim report card; starting a
    school newspaper)
- participation in a Teachers' Center (Mertens & Yarger, 1981; Rud & Oldendorf,
    1992)
- inquiry (Short, 1991; Tikunoff & Mergendoller, 1983)
- peer evaluations
- interview team for hiring new teacher or principal
- piloting or field testing a program
- leadership responsibility (e.g., staff development)
- reflective and reflexive thinking (Schon, 1983; Schon, 1987)
- transfer to a new grade or school (Hannay & Chism, 1988; Huberman, 1989)
- self-observation and analysis (Howey, Matthes, & Zimpher, 1987, p. 81)

APPENDIX D: Table D-1

Results from the OCDQ-RE Questionnaire

Climate Profile for Irene's[a] School (Open)		Climate Profile for Amy's School (Open)	
Principal's Behavior		**Principal's Behavior**	
Supportive Behavior	596 (High)	Supportive Behavior	699 (Very high)
Directive Behavior	271 (Very low)	Directive Behavior	427 (Low)
Restrictive Behavior	824 (Very high)	Restrictive Behavior	501 (Average)
Teachers' Behavior		**Teachers' Behavior**	
Collegial Behavior	645 (Very high)	Collegial Behavior	570 (High)
Intimate Behavior	489 (Slightly below average)	Intimate Behavior	583 (High)
Disengaged Behavior	343 (Very low)	Disengaged Behavior	502 (Average)
Openness of Principal Behavior	501 (Average)	Openness of Principal Behavior	590 (High)
Openness of Teacher Behavior	597 (High)	Openness of Teacher Behavior	551 (High)

TableD-1 (continued)

Climate Profile for Camille's School (Open)		Climate Profile for Donna's School (Bordering on Disengaged)	
Principal's Behavior		Principal's Behavior	
Supportive Behavior	617 (Very high)	Supportive Behavior	411 (Low)
Directive Behavior	239 (Very low)	Directive Behavior	333 (Very low)
Restrictive Behavior	308 (Very low)	Restrictive Behavior	630 (Very high)
Teachers' Behavior		Teachers' Behavior	
Collegial Behavior	756 (Very high)	Collegial Behavior	496 (Average)
Intimate Behavior	676 (Very high)	Intimate Behavior	723 (Very high)
Disengaged Behavior	264 (Very low)	Disengaged Behavior	740 (Very high)
Openness of Principal Behavior	690 (Very high)	Openness of Principal Behavior	482 (Slightly below average)
Openness of Teacher Behavior	723 (Very high)	Openness of Teacher Behavior	493 (Average)

Table D-1 (continued)

Climate Profile for Elizabeth's School (Disengaged)		Climate Profile for Mary's School (Open)	
Principal's Behavior		Principal's Behavior	
Supportive Behavior	658 (Very high)	Supportive Behavior	617 (Very high)
Directive Behavior	458 (Below average)	Directive Behavior	271 (Very low)
Restrictive Behavior	437 (Low)	Restrictive Behavior	630 (Very high)
Teachers' Behavior		Teachers' Behavior	
Collegial Behavior	273 (Very low)	Collegial Behavior	719 (Very high)
Intimate Behavior	443 (Low)	Intimate Behavior	910 (Very high)
Disengaged Behavior	660 (Very high)	Disengaged Behavior	581 (High)
Openness of Principal Behavior	588 (High)	Openness of Principal Behavior	572 (High)
Openness of Teacher Behavior	352 (Very low)	Openness of Teacher Behavior	683 (Very high)

Note. This questionnaire represents teachers' perceptions of their present school climate. The scores for the instrument were standardized against the normative data provided by a New Jersey sample, with the average score being 490-510. The four typologies of school climates include open (open principal and teacher behavior), closed (closed principal but open teacher behavior), engaged (closed principal behavior but open teacher behavior), and disengaged (open principal behavior but closed teacher behavior). For details, see Hoy, Tarter, and Kottkamp (1991).

[a]Irene had been at the school only five weeks when she did the questionnaire. She did not feel that she knew the staff and principal well enough to provide more than an initial impression.

NOTES

[1]Pseudonyms have been used throughout the study, both for participants and for the schools in their district.

[2]Grade Point Average (GPA) is an American system of standardizing college scores. The highest possible GPA is 4.0. Honors standing generally includes scores of 3.5 and higher.

BIBLIOGRAPHY

Ashton, P., & Webb, R. (1986). *Making a difference: Teachers' sense of efficacy and student achievement.* New York: Longman, Inc.

Ball, S., & Goodson, I. (Eds.). (1985). *Teachers' lives and careers.* Philadelphia: The Falmer Press.

Barnes, H. (1989). Cited in K. Howey & N. Zimpher, *Profiles of preservice teacher education: Inquiry into the nature of programs* (pp.216-217). Albany, NY: State University of New York Press.

Barnes, H., & Putnam, J. (1981, February). *Professional development through reciprocity and reflection.* Paper presented at the Annual Meeting of the American Association of Colleges for Teacher Education, Detroit, MI.

Berliner, D. (1986, August-September). In pursuit of the expert pedogogue. *Educational Researcher, 15*(7), 5-13.

Berman, L. (1987). The teacher as decision maker. In F. Bolin & J. M. Falk (Eds.), *Teacher renewal: Professional issues, personal choices* (pp. 202-216). New York: Teachers College Press.

Bogdan, R., & Biklen, S. (1992). *Qualitative research for education: An introduction to theory and methods* (2nd ed.). Boston: Allyn and Bacon.

Bolin, F. (1987). Reassessment and renewal in teaching. In F. Bolin & J. M. Falk (Eds.), *Teacher renewal: Professional issues, personal choices* (pp. 6-16). New York: Teachers College Press.

154

Bolin, F., & Falk, J. M. (Eds.). (1987). *Teacher renewal: Professional issues, personal choices*. New York: Teachers College Press.

Bryant, B. (1981). A review of the literature in selected areas of educational research. In T. Andrews, W. R. Houston, & B. Bryant (Eds.), *Adult learners (A research study)* (pp. 41-68). Washington, DC: Association of Teacher Educators.

Burke, P., & Heideman, R. (Eds.). (1985). *Career-long teacher education*. Springfield, IL: Charles C. Thomas, Publisher.

Campbell, K. (1988). Adaptive strategies of experienced expert teachers: A grounded theory study (Doctoral dissertation, The University of Nebraska - Lincoln, 1988). *Dissertation Abstracts International, 50*, 03A.

Campbell, K. (1990-91, Winter). Personal norms of experienced expert suburban high school teachers: Implications for selecting and retaining outstanding individuals. *Action in Teacher Education, 12*(4), 35-40.

Carnegie Task Force on Teaching as a Profession. (1986). *A nation prepared: Teachers for the 21st century*. New York: Carnegie Forum on Education and the Economy.

Chambers, J. H. (1983). *The achievement of education: An examination of key concepts in educational practice*. New York: Harper & Row, Publishers, Inc.

Christensen, J. (1985). Adult learning and teacher career stage development. In P. Burke & R. Heideman (Eds.), *Career-long teacher education* (pp. 158-180). Springfield, IL: Charles C. Thomas, Publisher.

Clark, C., & Peterson, P. (1986). Teachers' thought processes. In M. Wittrock (Ed.), *Handbook of research on teaching* (3rd ed.) (pp. 255-296). New York: Macmillan Publishing Company.

Clay, M. (1991). *Becoming literate: The construction of inner control*. Portsmouth, NH: Heinemann Educational Books, Inc.

Cohn, M. (1992). How teachers perceive teaching: Change over two decades, 1964-1984. In A. Lieberman (Ed.), *The changing contexts of teaching: The ninety-first yearbook of the National Society for the Study of Education* (pp. 110-137). Chicago: University of Chicago Press.

Collinson, V. (1992). [Professional Development Activities for Teachers]. Unpublished raw data.

Denzin, N. (1989). *The research act: A theoretical introduction to sociological methods* (3rd ed.). Englewood Cliffs, NJ: Prentice-Hall.

Dewey, J. (1899/1976). *The school and society.* Carbondale, IL: Southern Illinois University Press.

Dewey, J. (1904/1965). The relation of theory to practice in education. In M. Borrowman, *Teacher education in America: A documentary history* (pp. 140-171). New York: Teachers College Press.

Dewey, J. (1916/1966). *Democracy and education.* New York: Macmillan Publishing Company.

Dewey, J. (1929). *The sources of a science of education.* New York: Liveright.

Dewey, J. (1933/1960). *How we think: A restatement of the relation of reflective thinking to the educative process.* Lexington, MA: D. C. Heath & Company.

Dewey, J. (1938). *Experience and education.* New York: Macmillan Publishing Company.

Dieter, D. (1975, November). *How outstanding teachers view themselves as persons.* Paper presented at the Annual Meeting of NCSTA, Charlotte, NC.

Easterly, J. (1983, October). *Perceptions of outstanding elementary teachers about themselves and their profession* (Tech. Rep. No. 1). Rochester, MI: Oakland University, The School of Human and Educational Services.

156

Edelfelt, R., & Lawrence, G. (1975). In-service education: The state of the art. In R. Edelfelt & M. Johnson (Eds.), *Rethinking in-service education* (pp. 1-23). Washington, DC: National Education Association.

Ellett, C., Loup, K., Evans, L., & Chauvin, S. (1992, April). *How valid are teacher nominations of superior colleagues?: An investigation using comprehensive, classroom-based assessments of teaching and learning.* Paper presented at the Annual Meeting of the American Educational Research Association, San Francisco, CA.

Ellis, N. (1984, April). *The work-life experience of teachers and orientation toward professional growth and development.* Paper presented at the Annual Meeting of the American Educational Research Association, New Orleans, LA.

Family Word Finder: A new thesaurus of synonyms and antonyms in dictionary form. (1975). Montreal: The Reader's Digest Association Ltd.

Feiman-Nemser, S., & Floden, R. (1986). The cultures of teaching. In M. Wittrock (Ed.), *Handbook of research on teaching* (3rd ed.) (pp. 505-526). New York: Macmillan Publishing Company.

Fetterman, D. (1989). *Ethnography step by step.* Newbury Park, CA: SAGE Publications, Inc.

Fielding, G. D., & Schalock, H. (1985). *Promoting the professional development of teachers and administrators.* Eugene, OR: Center for Educational Policy and Management, University of Oregon.

Fosnot, C. T. (1989). *Enquiring teachers, enquiring learners: A constructivist approach for teaching.* New York: Teachers College Press.

Fullan, M., & Hargreaves, A. (1992). Teacher development and educational change. In M. Fullan & A. J. Hargreaves (Eds.), *Teacher development and educational change* (pp. 1-9). London: The Falmer Press.

Gardner, H. (1991). *The unschooled mind: How children think and how schools should teach.* New York: Basic Books.

157

Gardner, J. W. (1963/1981). *Self-renewal: The individual and the innovative society.* New York: W. W. Norton & Company.

Gibbons, M., & Norman, P. (1987). An integrated model for sustained staff development. In M. Wideen & I. Andrews (Eds.), *Staff development for school improvement: A focus on the teacher* (pp. 103-128). Philadelphia: The Falmer Press.

Gibson, S., & Dembo, M. H. (1984, August). Teacher efficacy: A construct validation. *Journal of Educational Psychology, 76*(4), 569-582.

Gilligan, C. (1982). *In a different voice: Psychological theory and women's development.* Cambridge, MA: Harvard University Press.

Goetz, J., & LeCompte, M. (1981, Spring). Ethnographic research and the problem of data reduction. *Anthropology and Education Quarterly, 12*(1), 51-70.

Goode, W., & Hatt, P. (1952). *Methods in social research.* New York: McGraw-Hill.

Goodlad, J. (1983). The school as workplace. In G. Griffin (Ed.), *Staff development: The eighty-second yearbook of the National Society for the Study of Education* (pp. 36-61). Chicago: The University of Chicago Press.

Goodlad, J. (1984). *A place called school: Prospects for the future.* New York: McGraw-Hill Book Company.

Goodlad, J. (Ed.). (1987). *The ecology of school renewal: The eighty-sixth yearbook of the National Society for the Study of Education.* Chicago: The University of Chicago Press.

Goodlad, J., Soder, R., & Sirotnik, K. (Eds.). (1990). *The moral dimensions of teaching.* San Francisco: Jossey-Bass Publishers.

Goodson, I. (Ed.). (1992). *Studying teachers' lives.* New York: Teachers College Press.

Green, T. (1971). *The activities of teaching.* New York: McGraw-Hill, Inc.

158

Greene, M. (1987). Teaching as project: Choice, perspective, and the public space. In F. Bolin & J. M. Falk (Eds.), *Teacher renewal: Professional issues, personal choices* (pp. 178-189). New York: Teachers College Press.

Griffin, G. (1983). Introduction: The work of staff development. In G. Griffin (Ed.), *Staff development: The eighty-second yearbook of the National Society for the Study of Education* (pp. 1-12). Chicago: The University of Chicago Press.

Grimmett, P., & Crehan, E. P. (1992). The nature of collegiality in teacher development: The case of clinical supervision. In M. Fullan & A. Hargreaves (Eds.), *Teacher development and educational change* (pp. 56-85). London: The Falmer Press.

Grundy, S. (1987). *Curriculum: Product or praxis?* Philadelphia: The Falmer Press.

Hannay, L., & Chism, N. (1988, Winter). The potential of teacher transfer in fostering professional development. *Journal of Curriculum and Supervision, 3*(2), 122-135.

Hargreaves, A. (1993). Individualism and individuality: Reinterpreting the teacher culture. In J. W. Little & M. W. McLaughlin (Eds.), *Teachers' work: Individuals, colleagues, and contexts* (pp. 51-76). New York: Teachers College Press.

Hargreaves, A., & Dawe, R. (1990). Paths of professional development: Contrived collegiality, collaborative culture, and the case of peer coaching. *Teaching and Teacher Education, 6*(3), 227-241.

Heath, D. H. (1980). Toward teaching as a self-renewing calling. In G. Hall, S. Hord, & G. Brown (Eds.), *Exploring issues in teacher education: Questions for future research* (pp. 291-306). Austin, TX: Research and Development Center for Teacher Education, University of Texas.

Holly, M. L. (1983). Staff development and adult learners. In *Staff development leadership: A resource book* (pp. 19-26). Columbus, OH: Ohio Department of Education.

Holmes Group. (1986). *Tomorrow's teachers: A report of the Holmes Group.* East Lansing, MI: Author.

Holmes Group. (1990). *Tomorrow's schools: Principles for the design of professional development schools.* East Lansing, MI: Author.

Howey, K. (1985, January-February). Six major functions of staff development: An expanded imperative. *Journal of Teacher Education, 36*(1), 58-64.

Howey, K., Bents, R., & Corrigan, D. (Eds.). (1981). *School-focused inservice: Descriptions and discussions.* Reston, VA: Association of Teacher Educators.

Howey, K., Matthes, W., & Zimpher, N. (1987). *Issues and problems in professional development.* Elmhurst, IL: North Central Regional Educational Laboratory.

Howey, K., & Strom, S. (1987). Teacher selection reconsidered. In M. Haberman & J. Backus (Eds.), *Advances in teacher education* (Vol. 1, pp. 3-30). Norwood, NJ: Ablex Publishing Corporation.

Howey, K., & Zimpher, N. (1989). *Profiles of preservice teacher education: Inquiry into the nature of programs.* Albany, NY: State University of New York Press.

Hoy, W., Tarter, C. J., & Kottkamp, R. (1991). *Open schools/healthy schools: Measuring organizational climate.* Newbury Park, CA: SAGE Publications, Inc.

Huberman, M. (1989, Fall). The professional life cycle of teachers. *Teachers College Record, 91*(1), 31-57.

Huberman, M. (1993). The model of the independent artisan in teachers' professional relations. In J. W. Little & M. W. McLaughlin (Eds.), *Teachers' work: Individuals, colleagues, and contexts* (pp.11-50). New York: Teachers College Press.

Huebner, D. (1987). The vocation of teaching. In F. Bolin & J. M. Falk (Eds.), *Teacher renewal: Professional issues, personal choices* (pp. 17-29). New York: Teachers College Press.

INTASC. (1992, September 1). *Model standards for beginning teacher licensing and development: A resource for state dialogue.* Interstate New Teacher Assessment and Support Consortium.

Jackson, P. (1968/1990). *Life in classrooms.* New York: Teachers College Press.

Jackson, P. (1987). The future of teaching. In F. Bolin & J. M. Falk (Eds.), *Teacher renewal: Professional issues, personal choices* (pp. 43-158). New York: Teachers College Press.

Joyce, B. (1984, Winter). Dynamic disequilibrium: The intelligence of growth. *Theory into Practice, 23*(1), 26-34.

Joyce, B., Hersh, R., & McKibbin, M. (1983). *The structure of school improvement.* New York: Longman, Inc.

Joyce, B., & Showers, B. (1980). Improving inservice training: The messages of research. *Educational Leadership, 37*(5), 379-385.

Joyce, B., & Showers, B. (1983). *Power in staff development through research on teaching.* Alexandria, VA: Association for Supervision and Curriculum Development.

Joyce, B., & Showers, B. (1988). *Student achievement through staff development.* New York: Longman, Inc.

Kaestle, C. (1993, January-February). The awful reputation of educational research. *Educational Researcher, 22*(1), 23-31.

Kanter, R. M. (1981). Career growth and organization power: Issues for educational management in the 1980s. *Teachers College Record, 82*(4), 553-566.

Katz, L., & Raths, J. (1985). Dispositions as goals for teacher education. *Teaching & Teacher Education, 1*(4), 301-307.

Kemmis, S. (1987). Critical reflection. In M. Wideen & I. Andrews (Eds.), *Staff development for school improvement: A focus on the teacher* (pp. 73-90). Philadelphia: The Falmer Press.

Kidd, J. R. (1976). *How adults learn.* New York: Association Press.

Knowles, M. (1978). *The adult learner: A neglected species* (2nd ed.). Houston, TX: Gulf Publishing.

Kottkamp, R. (1990). Teacher attitudes about work. In P. Reyes (Ed.), *Teachers and their workplace: Commitment, performance, and productivity* (pp. 86-114). Newbury Park, CA: SAGE Publications, Inc.

Krupp, J. A. (1981). *Adult development: Implications for staff development.* Colchester, CT: Project RISE.

Kvale, S. (1989). To validate is to question. In S. Kvale (Ed.), *Issues of validity in qualitative research* (pp. 73-92). Sweden: Studentlitterature.

Leggett, D., & Hoyle, S. (1987). Peer coaching: One district's experience in using teachers as staff developers. *Journal of Staff Development, 8*(1), 16-20.

Leithwood, K. (1990). The principal's role in teacher development. In B. Joyce (Ed.), *Changing school culture through staff development* (pp. 71-90). Washington, DC: Association for Supervision and Curriculum Development.

Lieberman, A. (Ed.). (1988). *Building a professional culture in schools.* New York: Teachers College Press.

Lieberman, A., & Rosenholtz, S. (1987). The road to school improvement: Barriers and bridges. In J. Goodlad (Ed.), *The ecology of school renewal: The eighty-sixth yearbook of the National Society for the Study of Education* (pp. 79-98). Chicago: The University of Chicago Press.

Lieberman, A., Saxl, E., & Miles, M. (1988). Teacher leadership: Ideology and practice. In A. Lieberman (Ed.), *Building a professional culture in schools* (pp. 148-166). New York: Teachers College Press.

Lincoln, Y., & Guba, E. (1985). *Naturalistic inquiry.* Newbury Park, CA: SAGE Publications, Inc.

Lincoln, Y., & Guba, E. (1989). *Fourth generation evaluation.* Newbury Park, CA: SAGE Publications, Inc.

Little, J. W. (1982, Fall). Norms of collegiality and experimentation: Workplace conditions of school success. *American Educational Research Journal, 19*(3), 325-340.

Little, J. W. (1987). Teachers as colleagues. In V. Richardson-Koehler (Ed.), *Educators' handbook: A research perspective* (pp. 491-518). New York: Longman, Inc.

Little, J. W. (1989). *The persistence of privacy: Autonomy and initiative in teachers' professional relations.* Paper presented at the Annual Meeting of the American Educational Research Association, San Francisco, CA.

Little, J. W. (1990). The mentor phenomenon and the social organization of teaching. *Review of Research in Education, 16*, 297-351.

Little, J. W. (1992a). Opening the black box of professional community. In A. Lieberman (Ed.), *The changing contexts of teaching: The ninety-first yearbook of the National Society for the Study of Education* (pp. 157-178). Chicago: The University of Chicago Press.

Little, J. W. (1992b). Teacher development and educational policy. In M. Fullan & A. Hargreaves (Eds.), *Teacher development and educational change* (pp. 170-193). London: The Falmer Press.

Little, J. W., & McLaughlin, M. W. (1993). Perspectives on cultures and contexts of teaching. In J. W. Little & M. W. McLaughlin (Eds.), *Teachers' work: Individuals, colleagues, and contexts* (pp. 1-8). New York: Teachers College Press.

Lortie, D. (1975). *Schoolteacher: A sociological study.* Chicago: The University of Chicago Press.

Louis, K. S. (1992). Restructuring and the problem of teachers' work. In A. Lieberman (Ed.), *The changing contexts of teaching: The ninety-first yearbook of the National Society for the Study of Education* (pp. 138-156). Chicago: University of Chicago Press.

Louis, K. S., & Smith, B. (1990). Teacher working conditions. In P. Reyes (Ed.), *Teachers and their workplace: Commitment, performance, and productivity* (pp. 23-47). Newbury Park, CA: SAGE Publications, Inc.

Marshall, C., & Rossman, G. (1989). *Designing qualitative research.* Newbury Park, CA: SAGE Publications, Inc.

McLaren, P. (1991). Field relations and the discourse of the other: Collaboration in our own ruin. In W. Shaffir & R. Stebbins (Eds.), *Experiencing fieldwork: An inside view of qualitative research* (pp. 149-163). Newbury Park, CA: SAGE Publications, Inc.

McLaughlin, M., & Marsh, D. (1978). Staff development and school change. *Teachers College Record, 80*(1), 69-94.

McLaughlin, M., & Yee, S. (1988). School as a place to have a career. In A. Lieberman (Ed.), *Building a professional culture in schools* (pp. 23-44). New York: Teachers College Press.

McNergney, R., Lloyd, J., Mintz, S., & Moore, J. (1988, September-October). Training for pedagogical decision making. *Journal of Teacher Education, 39*(5), 37-43.

Merriam, S. (1988). *Case study research in education: A qualitative approach.* San Francisco: Jossey-Bass Publishers.

Mertens, S., & Yarger, S. (1981). *Teachers centers in action: A comprehensive study of program activities, staff services, resources and policy board operations in 37 federally-funded teacher centers.* New York: Syracuse Area Teacher Center.

Mertz, R. (1987). *Teaching as learning: The personal dimensions of teacher growth.* Columbus, OH: Ohio Department of Education.

Miles, M., & Huberman, A. M. (1984). *Qualitative data analysis: A sourcebook of new methods.* Newbury Park, CA: SAGE Publications, Inc.

Murphy, M. L. (1985). An analysis of teacher incentives and disincentives relative to teacher retention (Doctoral dissertation, University of Nevada, Reno, 1985). *Dissertation Abstracts International, 46*, 08A.

NASDTEC. (1992, July). *Washington outcome-based committee results.* National Association of State Directors of Teacher Education and Certification.

National Commission on Excellence in Education. (1983). *A nation at risk*. Washington, DC: Government Printing Office.

Noffke, S. (1990, October). *Research together: Curriculum inquiry with, not on, teachers*. Paper presented at the Bergamo Curriculum Conference, Dayton, OH.

Ohio State Department of Education. (1989-1990). *Teacher Development Program Evaluation Reports*. Columbus, OH: Author.

Ouchi, W. (1981). *Theory Z: How American business can meet the Japanese challenge*. Reading, MA: Addison-Wesley.

Owens, R. (1991). *Organizational behavior in education* (4th ed.). Englewood Cliffs, NJ: Prentice Hall.

Patton, M. (1990). *Qualitative evaluation and research methods* (2nd ed.). Newbury Park, CA: SAGE Publications, Inc.

Penick, J., Yager, R., & Bonstetter, R. (1986). Teachers make exemplary programs. *Educational Leadership, 44*(2), 14-20.

Peshkin, A. (1988, October). In search of subjectivity – one's own. *Educational Researcher, 17*(7), 17-21.

Peters, T. J., & Waterman, R., Jr. (1982). *In search of excellence: Lessons from America's best-run companies*. New York: Harper & Row, Publishers, Inc.

Rental, V. (1992, May). *Preparing clinical faculty: Research on teacher reasoning*. Paper presented at the Conference on Faculty Development, Washington, DC.

Resnick, L., & Klopfer, L. (1989). Toward the thinking curriculum: An overview. In L. Resnick & L. Klopfer (Eds.), *Toward the thinking curriculum: Current cognitive research* (pp. 1-18). Washington, DC: Association for Supervision and Curriculum Development.

Reyes, P. (Ed.). (1990). *Teachers and their workplace: Commitment, performance, and productivity*. Newbury Park, CA: SAGE Publications, Inc.

Reynolds, M. (Ed.). (1989). *Knowledge base for the beginning teacher.* Oxford: Pergamon Press.

Rosenholtz, S. (1989). *Teachers' workplace: The social organization of schools.* New York: Teachers College Press.

Rosenholtz, S., & Smylie, M. (1984, November). Teacher compensation and career ladders. *The Elementary School Journal, 85*(2), 149-166.

Ross, E. W., Cornett, J., & McCutcheon, G. (Eds.). (1992). *Teacher personal theorizing: Connecting curriculum practice, theory, and research.* Albany, NY: State University of New York Press.

Rud, A., Jr., & Oldendorf, W. (Eds.). (1992). *A place for teacher renewal: Challenging the intellect, creating educational reform.* New York: Teachers College Press.

Samson, R. (1965). *The mind builder.* New York: E. P. Dutton & Co., Inc.

Sarason, S. (1971). *The culture of the school and the problem of change.* Boston: Allyn & Bacon.

Sarason, S. (1990). *The predictable failure of educational reform: Can we change course before it's too late?* San Francisco: Jossey-Bass Publishers.

Scheffler, I. (1991). *In praise of the cognitive emotions.* New York: Routledge.

Schlechty, P., & Vance, V. (1983). Recruitement, selection, and retention: The shape of the teaching force. *The Elementary School Journal, 83*(4), 469-487.

Schlechty, P., & Whitford, B. L. (1983). The organizational context of school systems and the functions of staff development. In G. Griffin (Ed.), *Staff development: The eighty-second yearbook of the National Society for the Study of Education* (pp. 62-91). Chicago: The University of Chicago Press.

Schon, D. (1987). *Educating the reflective practitioner: Toward a new design for teaching and learning in the professions.* San Francisco: Jossey-Bass Publishers.

Sergiovanni, T. (1992). *Moral leadership: Getting to the heart of school improvement*. San Francisco: Jossey-Bass Publishers.

Shanoski, L., & Hranitz, J. (1989). *An analysis of characteristics of outstanding teachers and the criteria used by colleges and universities to select future teachers*. Paper presented at the Association of Teacher Educators Summer Workshop, Tacoma, WA.

Sherman, N. (1989). *The fabric of character: Aristotle's theory of virtue*. Oxford: Clarendon Press.

Schon, D. (1983). *The reflective practitioner: How professionals think in action*. New York: Basic Books.

Schon, D. (1987). *Educating the reflective practitioner*. San Francisco: Jossey-Bass Publishers.

Short, E. (Ed.). (1991). *Forms of curriculum inquiry*. Albany, NY: State University of New York Press.

Simmons, J., & Schuette, M. K. (1988, Summer). Strengthening teachers' reflective decision making. *Journal of Staff Development, 9*(3), 18-26.

Sizer, T. (1984). *Horace's compromise: The dilemma of the American high school*. Boston: Houghton Mifflin.

Smylie, M. (1990). Teacher efficacy at work. In P. Reyes (Ed.), *Teachers and their workplace: Commitment, performance, and productivity* (pp. 48-66). Newbury Park, CA: SAGE Publications, Inc.

Sprinthall, N., & Thies-Sprinthall, L. (1983). The teacher as an adult learner: A cognitive-developmental view. In G. Griffin (Ed.), *Staff development: The eighty-second yearbook of the National Society for the Study of Education* (pp. 13-35). Chicago: The University of Chicago Press.

Stake, R. (1978, February). The case study method in social inquiry. *Educational Researcher, 7*(2), 5-7.

Stake, R. (1988). Case study methods in educational research: Seeking sweet water. In R. Jaeger (Ed.), *Complementary methods for research in education* (pp. 253-273). Washington, DC: American Educational Research Association.

Stevenson, C. M. (1986). An investigation into the rewards in teaching for high-performing elementary school teachers (Doctoral dissertation, University of Colorado at Boulder, 1986). *Dissertation Abstracts International, 47*, 09A.

St. Maurice, H. (1990). A philosophical basis for staff development: A rhetorical approach. In P. Burke, R. Heideman, & C. Heideman (Eds.), *Programming for staff development: Fanning the flame* (pp. 10-41). Philadelphia: The Falmer Press.

Stoll, Louise. (1992). Teacher growth in the effective school. In M. Fullan & A. Hargreaves (Eds.), *Teacher development and educational change* (pp. 104-122). London: The Falmer Press.

Stone, I. (1987). A phenomenological study of significant life experiences of "Teachers of the Year" (Doctoral dissertation, United States International University, 1987). *Dissertation Abstracts International, 48*, 11A.

Talbert, J. (1993). Constructing a schoolwide professional community: The negotiated order of a performing arts school. In J. W. Little & M. W. McLaughlin (Eds.), *Teachers' work: Individuals, colleagues, and contexts* (pp. 164-184). New York: Teachers College Press.

Tatum, D. (1993). *Persuasive communication: Business and professional speaking*. Paper presented at the Annual Meeting of the American Educational Research Association, Atlanta, GA.

Thies-Sprinthall, L., & Sprinthall, N. (1987). Experienced teachers: Agents for revitalization and renewal as mentors and teacher educators. *Journal of Education, 169*(1), 65-79.

Tikunoff, W., & Mergendoller, J. (1983). Inquiry as a means to professional growth: The teacher as researcher. In G. Griffin (Ed.), *Staff development: The eighty-second yearbook of the National Society for the Study of Education* (pp. 210-227). Chicago: The University of Chicago Press.

Tom, A., & Valli, L. (1990). Professional knowledge for teachers. In W. R. Houston (Ed.), *Handbook of research on teacher education* (pp. 373-392). New York: Macmillan Publishing Company.

Valencia, S., & Killion, J. (1988, Spring). Overcoming obstacles to teacher change: Direction from school-based efforts. *The Journal of Staff Development, 9*(2), 2-8.

Van Schaack, H., & Glick, I. D. (1982, February). *A qualitative study of excellence in teaching and The search for excellence in teaching: An annotated bibliography.* Washington, DC: National Institute of Education, ERIC Clearinghouse on Teacher Education.

Vygotsky, L. (1978). *Mind in society: The development of higher psychological processes* (M. Cole, V. John-Steiner, S. Scribner, E. Souberman, Trans.). Cambridge, MA: Harvard University Press.

Walberg, H. (1990). Enhancing school productivity: The research basis. In P. Reyes (Ed.), *Teachers and their workplace: Commitment, performance, and productivity* (pp. 277-296). Newbury Park, CA: SAGE Publications, Inc.

Waller, W. (1965). *The sociology of teaching.* New York: John Wiley & Sons, Inc.

Wasley, P. (1991). *Teachers who lead: The rhetoric of reform and the realities of practice.* New York: Teachers College Press.

Watson, N., & Fullan, M. (1992). Beyond school district - university partnerships. In M. Fullan & A. Hargreaves (Eds.), *Teacher development and educational change* (pp. 213-242). Philadelphia: The Falmer Press.

Wax, R. (1971). *Doing fieldwork: Warnings and advice.* Chicago: The University of Chicago Press.

Webster's third new international dictionary, unabridged: The great library of the English language. (1976). Springfield, MA: Merriam-Webster.

Westerhoff, J. (1987). The teacher as pilgrim. In F. Bolin & J. M. Falk (Eds.), *Teacher renewal: Professional issues, personal choices* (pp. 190-201). New York: Teachers College Press.

Wigginton, B. E. (1985). *Sometimes a shining moment: The Foxfire experience.* Garden City, NY: Anchor Press/Doubleday.

Willie, R., & Howey, K. (1980). Reflections on adult development: Implications for inservice teacher education. In W. R. Houston & R. Pankratz (Eds.), *Staff development and educational change* (pp. 25-51). Reston, VA: Association of Teacher Educators.

Woods, P. (1986). *Inside schools: Ethnography in educational research.* London: Routledge and Kegan Paul.

Yarger, S., Howey, K., & Joyce, B. (1980). *Inservice teacher education.* Palo Alto, CA: Booksend Laboratory.

Yee, S. (1990). *Careers in the classroom: When teaching is more than a job.* New York: Teachers College Press.

Yonemura, M. (1982). Teacher conversations: A potential source of their own professional growth. *Curriculum Inquiry, 12*(3), 239-256.

Zeichner, K., & Grant, C. (1981, October). Biography and social structure in the socialization of student teacher: A re-examination of the pupil control ideologies of student teachers. *Journal of Education for Teaching, 7*(3), 299-314.

INDEX

A

Administrator 31, 46, 55, 93, 106, 107, 118, 119, 143, 144, 156
Ashton 14, 15, 34, 153
Attribute 3, 5, 18–21, 38, 45, 120, 126
Autonomy 11, 14, 22, 34, 36, 37, 118, 143, 162

B

Ball 2, 27, 153
Barnes 73, 88, 153
Belief 1, 2, 5, 7, 22, 23, 29, 32, 33, 36, 50, 52, 62, 73, 81, 85–87, 95, 98, 113, 119, 124, 126, 127, 131, 137, 138, 140, 141, 142, 143, 146
Beliefs
  about teaching 4, 55, 56, 73, 86, 95, 119, 122, 129, 135, 140, 142, 143, 146
Berliner 23, 52, 153
Berman 35, 95, 105, 153
Biklen 41, 46, 48, 153
Biographies 4, 27, 32, 58, 65, 132–136
Biography 2, 169
Bogdan 41, 46, 48, 153
Bolin 6, 12, 18, 27, 153, 154, 158–160, 169
Bonstetter 2, 10, 11, 21, 164
Bryant 28, 154
Burke 139, 154, 167

C

Campbell 3, 6, 11, 22, 27, 34, 37, 85, 98, 121, 154
Care 2, 9, 12, 16, 18, 20, 21–23, 25, 29, 30, 35, 37–39, 49, 56, 63, 67, 76, 78, 82, 84–86, 95, 110, 118–124, 126, 127, 129, 133, 142
Carnegie 1, 4, 154
Certainty 13, 15, 20, 25, 32–35, 96
Chambers 139, 154
Characteristics 2, 3, 16, 21, 22, 29, 35, 38, 39, 41, 42, 45, 120, 126, 166
Chauvin 6, 22, 45, 156
Chism 148, 158
Christensen 28, 135, 154
Clark 23, 43, 154
Clay 7, 154
Climate 1, 5, 8, 13, 14, 21, 27, 28, 30, 32, 34, 35, 39, 41, 47, 48, 50, 105, 109, 113, 116–119, 146, 159
Cohn 141, 155
Collaboration 29, 31, 32, 34–38, 47, 72, 163
Collegiality 23, 31, 35, 36, 49, 99, 104, 105, 109, 117, 140, 143, 145, 146, 148–151, 158, 162
Commitment 2, 3, 5, 7–10, 12, 14, 19, 20–23, 29, 30, 32–37, 39, 56, 65, 96, 120, 123, 124, 126, 129, 133, 143, 161, 163, 165, 166, 168
Constraint 4, 56, 99, 115, 116, 118, 146
Cornett 25, 165
Creativity 8, 10, 11, 20, 23, 29, 30, 37, 38, 114, 138

Credibility 49, 51, 96, 97, 99, 118
Crehan 36, 158
Culture 1, 3, 8, 18, 23, 32, 35, 107, 156, 158, 161–163, 165
Curiosity 7, 10–13, 19, 20, 57
Curriculum 19, 22, 24, 37, 44, 50, 62, 67, 69, 72, 79, 81, 83, 86, 89, 93, 96, 104, 108, 123, 127, 128, 131, 134, 135, 138, 146, 147, 158, 160, 161, 164–166, 169

D

Dawe 36, 158
Decision making 9, 15, 16, 27, 30, 34, 44, 86, 146, 163, 166
Dembo 34, 157
Denzin 42, 46, 47, 155
Development 4, 7, 8, 10, 17, 18, 23–28, 34, 42, 47, 74, 85, 89, 97, 100, 123, 128, 138, 140, 154, 156–158, 160, 161, 164, 166, 168, 169
  cognitive 12, 24, 25, 29, 34, 89, 138
  conceptual 28
  human 25, 30
  moral 12, 28
  pedagogical 24, 89, 140
  personal 23
  professional 2, 4, 5–7, 10, 21, 23, 24, 26, 27, 29, 31, 32, 35, 47, 51, 56, 73, 88, 89, 104, 126–129, 137, 139, 145–147, 153, 155, 156, 158, 159
  psychological 13, 24, 29
  social 31
  staff 7, 18, 23, 24, 26, 27, 88, 114, 148, 157–161, 163, 165–169
  teacher 3–5, 8, 11, 12, 21, 23, 24, 26, 27, 39, 41, 156, 158, 161, 162, 164, 167, 168
  theoretical 24, 25, 34, 98, 138, 140
Dewey 6, 7, 12, 13, 17, 19, 20, 25, 33, 38, 87, 132, 134, 137, 139, 140, 142, 155
Dieter 2, 6, 155
Disposition 3, 5, 8, 12, 13, 17–21, 25, 31, 35, 38, 39, 64, 65, 86, 120, 131–136, 138, 139, 142, 143, 160
District support 99, 103, 114, 146

E

Easterly 2, 6, 10, 11, 21, 45, 155
Edelfelt 23, 156
Efficacy 3, 11, 14, 15, 22, 27, 31, 33, 34, 37, 96, 153, 157, 166
Ellett 6, 22, 45, 156

Ellis 5, 156
Evans 6, 22, 45, 156
Exemplary 2–8, 10, 11, 21–23, 28, 29, 34, 37–39, 41, 42, 44–46, 52–56, 61, 73, 85, 87, 99, 116, 119, 120, 126, 128, 129, 131–133, 135–138, 142–144, 164

F

Factor 1, 2, 3, 4, 23, 27, 34, 49, 50, 56, 93, 99, 103, 111, 114, 115, 117, 118, 129, 143
Factors
  constraining 49, 145, 146
  enabling 49, 145, 146
  organizational 4, 41, 42, 99
Falk 27, 153, 154, 158–160, 169
Feiman-Nemser 23, 156
Fetterman 43, 156
Fielding 23, 156
Flexibility 11, 20, 25, 29, 46, 72, 76, 86, 110, 111, 118
Floden 23, 156
Formative experiences 4, 51, 56, 58, 129
Fosnot 23, 137, 156
Fullan 4, 8, 12, 27, 156, 158, 162, 167, 168

G

Gardner 8–10, 16–20, 24, 25, 29, 35, 38, 39, 41, 85, 102, 105, 123, 126, 131, 134, 141, 142, 156, 157
Gibbons 8, 12, 157
Gibson 34, 157
Gilligan 22, 157
Glick 2, 6, 10, 11, 21, 22, 45, 168
Goetz 43, 48, 157
Goode 42, 157
Goodlad 1, 5, 7, 16, 25, 31, 35, 36, 119, 157, 161
Goodson 2, 27, 41, 58, 153, 157
Grant 2, 109, 169
Green 12, 18, 19, 58, 157, 158
Greene 12
Griffin 23, 157, 158, 165, 166, 168
Grimmett 36, 158
Grundy 26, 158
Guba 41, 42, 48–51, 161, 162

H

Hannay 148, 158
Hargreaves 4, 14, 27, 31, 32, 36–38, 156, 158, 162, 167, 168

Hatt 42, 157
Heath 12, 13, 24, 25, 30, 31, 155, 158
Heideman 139, 154, 167
Hersh 2, 12, 160
Holly 27, 28, 158
Holmes 1, 4, 23, 27, 159
Howey 12, 13, 18, 23–26, 29, 30, 34, 41, 72, 89, 103, 134, 139, 140, 148, 153, 159, 169
Hoy 5, 14, 23, 35, 47, 109, 159, 161
Hranitz 10, 11, 21, 45, 166
Huberman 28, 43, 46, 48, 51, 97, 126, 148, 159, 163
Huebner 12, 18, 106, 159

I

Innovation 3, 10, 11, 14–17, 19, 20, 27, 31, 33, 34, 36–38, 44, 73, 86, 118, 128, 147
Inquiry 4, 9, 13, 16, 23, 25, 26, 38, 42, 51, 73, 86, 89, 98, 99, 131, 136–139, 142, 143, 148, 153, 159, 161, 164, 166–169
INTASC 134, 160
Interaction 1, 8, 12, 22, 28, 30, 35–37, 41, 48, 68, 73, 109, 119, 126, 135
  collegial 3, 27, 37, 72
  human 15, 17–19, 24, 35, 38, 41, 86, 97, 122, 126, 137, 143
  professional 14, 31, 109
  social 5, 8, 18, 20, 23, 38, 59, 89, 103, 109, 119, 123, 126
Involvement 3, 4, 8, 33, 56, 64, 85, 93, 95–98, 116, 117, 124, 126, 135, 138, 141–143
Isolation 5, 31, 32, 35–37, 97, 126

J

Jackson 6, 13, 19, 21, 25, 43, 44, 98, 160
Joyce 2, 12, 13, 17, 20, 22, 23, 27, 34, 38, 103, 147, 160, 161, 169
Judgment 13, 19, 20, 25, 26, 33, 37, 43, 44, 49, 52, 106, 111, 131, 135, 139, 142

K

Kaestle 25, 160
Kanter 14, 30, 160
Katz 5, 160
Kemmis 8, 12, 160
Kidd 28, 161
Killion 12, 28, 168
Klopfer 12, 17, 19, 20, 23, 85, 164
Knowles 28, 161

Kottkamp 5, 14, 34, 35, 47, 109, 159, 161
Krupp 28, 161
Kvale 49, 51, 161

L

Learners 2, 3, 7, 28, 34, 35, 38, 45, 52, 73, 78, 85, 107, 135, 139, 140, 154, 156, 158
Learning 2–6, 8, 13, 14, 17–20, 22, 23, 25,–30, 32–38, 43, 45, 52, 53, 55, 56, 59, 61, 62, 64, 65, 67–69, 71– 76, 78–83, 85–89, 92, 94–99, 103, 104, 107, 117–120, 122–124, 126–129, 132, 134–137, 139, 140, 142, 143, 154, 156, 163, 166
  continuous 9, 10, 12, 14, 22, 29, 39, 86, 87, 104, 119, 120, 133, 142
  holistic 86
  lifelong 16, 132, 135
  love of 2, 10, 23, 132, 135
  student 3, 14, 22, 25, 33, 95, 123, 140
  teacher 3, 72
LeCompte 43, 48, 157
Leggett 23, 161
Leithwood 12, 13, 24, 29, 95, 161
Lieberman 12, 14, 22–24, 31, 36, 155, 161–163
Lincoln 41, 42, 48–51, 161, 162
Little 3, 7, 14, 18, 22, 23, 26, 27, 31–33, 35, 36, 88, 96, 98, 158, 159, 162, 167
Lloyd 27, 163
Lortie 1, 2, 5, 12, 22, 23, 24, 33, 35, 64, 121, 126, 136, 162
Louis 14, 30, 31, 38, 103, 162, 163, 167
Loup 6, 22, 45, 156

M

Marsh 15, 34, 41, 42, 47, 163
Matthes 148, 159
McCutcheon 25, 165
McKibbin 2, 160
Mckibbin 12
McLaren 44, 163
McLaughlin 3, 12, 15, 22, 34, 36, 38, 103, 158, 159, 162, 163, 167
McNergney 27, 163
Mergendoller 23, 26, 148, 168
Merriam 42, 163, 169
Mertens 148, 163
Mertz 2, 10, 21, 24, 27, 37, 163
Miles 12, 22, 24, 35, 43, 46, 48, 51, 161, 163
Mintz 27, 163
Moore 27, 163

Motivation 1, 2, 8, 9, 12, 14, 16, 19, 20, 27, 33, 35, 83, 95, 123, 126, 133
Murphy 6, 163

N

NASDTEC 134, 164
Network 37, 48, 49, 92–98, 108, 109, 116–118, 129, 131, 145, 148
Noffke 44, 164
Norman 8, 12, 157

O

Oldendorf 27, 123, 148, 165
Ouchi 1, 164
Owens 1, 164

P

Parents 33–35, 38, 59–61, 63, 64, 66, 67, 70, 71, 74, 78, 82–86, 88, 92, 97, 99–101, 103, 104, 110, 111, 114, 121–123, 127, 132–134, 139, 141, 146, 147
Patton 43, 46, 47, 50, 164
Penick 2, 10, 11, 21, 22, 164
Peshkin 43, 164
Peters 1, 23, 43, 154, 164
Power 1, 3, 30, 32, 33, 38, 57, 98, 99, 105, 106, 108, 136, 141, 143, 160
Preservice 1, 4, 5, 23, 26, 27, 43, 65, 127, 129, 135–139, 153, 159
Principal 47, 50, 59, 86, 89, 96, 98–100, 103, 104, 106–114, 117–121, 124, 125, 128, 141, 142, 146, 148–150, 151, 161
Professionalism 36, 48, 95, 99, 103–105, 107, 119, 141, 142
Professionalization 1, 4, 23, 26
Putnam 88, 153

R

Raths 5, 160
Reflection 6, 13, 17, 19, 25, 26, 38, 47, 73, 86, 88, 89, 91, 92, 97, 135, 137, 138, 153, 160, 169
Relationships 3, 8, 11, 14, 21, 22, 29–35, 37, 41, 48, 58, 61, 62, 68, 95, 97, 99, 102, 104, 105, 109, 119, 123, 126, 145, 146
Renew 3–10, 14, 16–21, 24–26, 27, 29, 30–33, 35, 38, 39, 41, 42, 44, 45, 47, 49–51, 55, 56, 58, 59, 73, 75, 86–89, 91, 95–100, 102, 103, 106–110, 113–119, 123, 129, 131–135,
139, 140, 141–143, 145, 146, 153, 154, 157–161, 165, 167, 169
Renewing 132
Rental 27, 164
Resnick 12, 17, 19, 20, 23, 85, 164
Resource 2, 3, 21, 22, 26, 31, 32, 46, 52, 53, 55, 69, 86, 89, 90, 93, 94, 96–99, 103, 104, 108, 112, 114, 115, 117, 118, 127, 128, 131, 132, 136, 137, 143, 146, 147, 158, 160, 163
Respect 10, 14, 19, 22, 30, 31, 38, 48, 61, 72, 86, 96, 97, 99, 103, 104, 105, 106, 109, 118, 119, 122, 123, 127, 137, 141
Retention 4, 34, 94, 117, 131, 143, 163, 165
Rewards 3, 11, 12, 14, 22, 30, 33, 34, 37, 38, 96, 121, 122, 123, 126, 143, 167
Reyes 34, 35, 126, 161, 163, 165, 166, 168
Reynolds 23, 165
Risk 1, 8–10, 12–16, 18, 20, 21, 23, 24, 28, 30, 31, 33, 43, 72, 73, 77, 78, 86, 127, 135, 139, 164
Rosenholtz 3, 8, 14, 15, 31–37, 41, 72, 96, 105, 107, 118, 139, 161, 165
Ross 2, 25, 41, 42, 47, 163, 165
Rud 27, 123, 148, 165

S

Samson 138, 165
Sarason 5, 8, 14, 17, 25, 165
Saxl 12, 22, 24, 35, 161
Schalock 23, 156
Scheffler 142, 165
Schlechty 16, 133, 165
Schon 23, 26, 137, 148, 166
Schuette 27, 137, 166
Self-knowledge 9, 10, 14, 16, 18, 24, 30, 86
Sergiovanni 5, 166
Shanoski 10, 11, 21, 45, 166
Sherman 142, 166
Short 26, 148, 166
Shortcuts 20
Showers 23, 27, 38, 103, 147, 160
Simmons 27, 137, 166
Sizer 1, 166
Smith 14, 30, 31, 103, 163
Smylie 14, 15, 34, 37, 165, 166
Sprinthall 12, 28, 29, 147, 166, 167
St. Maurice 7, 167
Stake 42, 44, 46, 167
Stevenson 3, 6, 11, 22, 37, 167
Stoll 14, 31, 167

Stone 3, 10, 11, 20–22, 167
Strom 134, 139, 159

T

Talbert 12, 25, 167
Tarter 5, 14, 35, 47, 109, 159
Tatum 138, 167
Teacher 10–12, 14, 15, 158
Teacher selection 4, 132, 133, 139, 159
Team teaching 31, 38, 66, 67, 69, 71, 72, 95, 132, 135, 136, 141, 142
Thies-Sprinthall 12
Thies-Sprinthall 28, 147, 166, 167
Tikunoff 23, 26, 148, 168
Tom 23, 81, 159, 168
Transfer 24, 43, 49, 50, 53, 99, 108–113, 116, 118, 119, 124, 128, 143, 148, 158
Trust 25, 28, 30, 31, 37, 43, 44, 47, 49, 72, 107

U

Understanding of self 24, 30, 34, 89

V

Valencia 12, 28, 168
Valli 23, 168
Values 1, 5, 16, 17, 19, 29, 30, 64, 86, 111, 126, 135
Van Schaack 2, 6, 10, 21, 22, 45, 168
Vance 133, 165
Vygotsky 38, 168

W

Walberg 132, 168
Waller 119, 168
Wasley 23, 27, 35, 168
Waterman 1, 164
Watson 8, 12, 168
Wax 43, 168
Webb 14, 15, 34, 153
Westerhoff 52, 169
Whitford 16, 165
Wigginton 2, 10, 11, 37, 169
Willie 13, 29, 30, 103, 169
Wonder 10, 12, 18–20, 52, 53, 61, 64, 67, 74, 81, 92–94, 97, 100, 107, 113, 120, 122, 123, 136
Woods 2, 169
Work ethic 64, 65, 86, 104, 124, 134, 143

Workplace 1, 3, 4, 7, 8, 20, 30, 32–34, 36, 38, 96, 131, 143, 157, 161–163, 165, 166, 168

Y

Yager 2, 10, 11, 21, 164
Yarger 12, 23, 148, 163, 169
Yee 3, 8, 12, 22, 35, 38, 95, 96, 103, 140, 163, 169
Yonemura 147, 169

Z

Zeichner 2, 169
Zimpher 72, 148, 153, 159